BATMAN **GOTHAM AFTER MIDNIGHT**

BATMAN GOTHAM AFTER MIDNIGHT

STEVE NILES WRITER KELLEY JONES ARTIST
MICHELLE MADSEN COLORIST PAT BROSSEAU LETTERER
BATMAN CREATED BY BOB KANE

DAN DIDIO SVP – EXECUTIVE EDITOR MICHAEL SIGLAIN EDITOR – ORIGINAL SERIES
HARVEY RICHARDS ASSISTANT EDITOR GEORG BREWER VP – DESIGN & DC DIRECT CREATIVE
BOB HARRAS GROUP EDITOR – COLLECTED EDITIONS SEAN MACKIEWICZ EDITOR
ROBBIN BROSTERMAN DESIGN DIRECTOR – BOOKS

DC COMICS
PAUL LEVITZ PRESIDENT & PUBLISHER RICHARD BRUNING SVP – CREATIVE DIRECTOR
PATRICK CALDON EVP – FINANCE & OPERATIONS AMY GENKINS SVP – BUSINESS & LEGAL AFFAIRS
JIM LEE EDITORIAL DIRECTOR – WILDSTORM GREGORY NOVECK SVP – CREATIVE AFFAIRS
STEVE ROTTERDAM SVP – SALES & MARKETING CHERYL RUBIN SVP – BRAND MANAGEMENT

COVER BY KELLEY JONES
PUBLICATION DESIGN BY ROBBIE BIEDERMAN

BATMAN: GOTHAM AFTER MIDNIGHT
PUBLISHED BY DC COMICS. COVER, TEXT AND COMPILATION COPYRIGHT © 2009 DC COMICS.
ALL RIGHTS RESERVED. ORIGINALLY PUBLISHED IN SINGLE MAGAZINE FORM IN BATMAN:
GOTHAM AFTER MIDNIGHT 1-12. COPYRIGHT © 2008, 2009 DC COMICS. ALL RIGHTS RESERVED.
ALL CHARACTERS, THEIR DISTINCTIVE LIKENESSES AND RELATED ELEMENTS FEATURED IN THIS
PUBLICATION ARE TRADEMARKS OF DC COMICS. THE STORIES, CHARACTERS AND INCIDENTS
FEATURED IN THIS PUBLICATION ARE ENTIRELY FICTIONAL. DC COMICS DOES NOT READ OR
ACCEPT UNSOLICITED SUBMISSIONS OF IDEAS, STORIES OR ARTWORK.

DC COMICS, 1700 BROADWAY, NEW YORK, NY 10019
A WARNER BROS. ENTERTAINMENT COMPANY
PRINTED IN CANADA. FIRST PRINTING.
ISBN: 978-1-4012-2238-3

SUSTAINABLE FORESTRY INITIATIVE
Certified Fiber Sourcing
www.sfiprogram.org
Fiber used in this product line meets the sourcing requirements
of the SFI program. www.sfiprogram.org PWC-SFICOC-260

INTRODUCTION BY JOHN CARPENTER

BATMAN HAS BEEN AROUND SINCE 1939, HAS BEEN REINVENTED BY EACH GENERATION OF COMIC BOOK CREATORS, AND DEFINITELY HAS THE BEST COSTUME OF ANY SUPERHERO EVER. FOR 70 YEARS THE DARK KNIGHT HAS WALKED TORTURED URBAN STREETS, BUT NEVER AS DARKLY AND STYLISHLY AS IN STEVE NILES AND KELLEY JONES'S HANDS.

GOTHAM AFTER MIDNIGHT IS AN ABSOLUTE BLAST. NILES'S SHARP NARRATIVE BLENDS HORROR, HUMOR, NOIR AND SWEEPING ACTION, AND HIS COLLABORATOR JONES IS SUCH A GIFTED ARTIST THAT YOU CAN'T STOP LOOKING AT THE PANELS. I'M AN ENORMOUS FAN OF THESE TWO GENTLEMEN. BATMAN COMIC BOOKS GET NO BETTER THAN THIS.

SO START TURNING THE PAGES. STEVE NILES AND KELLEY JONES WILL TRANSPORT YOU TO A GIDDY, BEAUTIFUL FEVER DREAM. I GUARANTEE IT.

JOHN CARPENTER IS THE VISIONARY FILM DIRECTOR RESPONSIBLE FOR MANY OF TODAY'S CULT CLASSICS, SUCH AS HALLOWEEN, ESCAPE FROM NEW YORK, THE THING, STARMAN, BIG TROUBLE IN LITTLE CHINA, AND MANY MORE.

FRIGHTENING
1
FIRST EPISODE
KELLEY JONES '08
BEWARE THE WITCHING HOUR

Chapter One

I remember the first time I said those words.

Gotham Antiquities & Rarities Exchange

Back then, there was a quiver in my voice.

Maybe I was a little scared.

Then.

YES! I FOUND YOU! THE *HAND* OF GLORY!

That was a long time ago.

I'm not afraid anymore.

DID YOU HEAR WHAT I SAID?

THE "BATMAN" THING. YEAH. WE'VE MET.

CLEARLY NOT, CRANE, BECAUSE YOU'RE STILL LIVING AS A COMMON LOWLIFE, BOTTOM-FEEDING, PIECE OF SCUM.

I'M ANYTHING *BUT* COMMON.

READ STATISTICS ON THE RISE OF THE CRIMINALLY INSANE WHILE YOU'RE LOCKED UP AT ARKHAM. YOU'D BE SURPRISED HOW COMMON YOU ARE.

WHAT'S THAT?

N...NOTHING.

No gas, no fight. I've always classified Crane as a revenge-seeking sociopath.

MATCHES? ON THE SCARECROW?

WHAT CAN I SAY...

AND MY TOLERANCE FOR PETTY CRIME IS AT AN ALL-TIME LOW!

CRUNCH!

HOW'S *YOUR* TOLERANCE, CRANE?

NOOOOOO!

AHHHHHHHHHHHH!

WHAT'S THE MATTER? WHAT ARE YOU AFRAID OF?

AHHHHHHHHHHHH!

WHY WERE YOU STEALING THE HAND, CRANE?

NO! STOP! STAY-- STAY AWAY FROM ME!

Criminals are a cowardly and superstitious lot.

But they are also predictable...so why has Scarecrow changed his M.O.?

WEEE-OOO WEEE-OOO

Twelve minutes. A little slow for Gotham's Finest.

SEE YOU AROUND, CRANE.

Chapter Two

Gotham City after dark is a dangerous place. Gotham City after midnight is Hell on Earth.

I've known that since the day I donned this cape and cowl.

LOOK AT THIS. YOU THINK THIS IS WHAT HE WAS AFTER?

A DRIED-UP OLD HAND? MAYBE. WHO KNOWS WITH THESE NUTS.

...HOW'D I GET HERE? WHO ARE YOU PEOPLE?

Like a disease or force of nature, crime has symptoms and patterns, and even though the individual may attempt to change or even cure what drives, the disease always wins.

You can't fault a disease any more than you can fault a snowstorm.

But when snow comes during the summer...

Or a disease changes course...

That's when I worry.

I'M GOING AHEAD TO MAKE SURE THEY DON'T SHIP HIM OFF TO ARKHAM BEFORE I'VE HAD A CHANCE TO QUESTION HIM. FINISH UP HERE AND CALL IN WHEN YOU'RE DONE.

I'LL SEE YOU BACK AT THE STATION HOUSE, BARRY.

Criminals, like Scarecrow, are locked into patterns. They have diseased minds. They can't help it.

16

But Scarecrow changed his pattern.

One, Crane doesn't do petty thefts, let alone stealing supernatural artifacts. His angle is vengeance and power over those who he believes wronged him.

Who wronged him can change day to day because he's psychotic.

Two, Crane always updates his Fear Gas. He knows I can build up a resistance. We've danced that dance for years.

Why didn't he this time?

The pack of matches. The address.

It might as well be a snare-trap set in plain sight.

FWOOSH

AXEMAN HAS ALREADY CLAIMED TWO VICTIMS. ROBBERY SEEMS TO BE THE MOTIVATION.

I WAS UNDER THE IMPRESSION HE THOUGHT OF HIMSELF AS SOME KIND OF HERO.

WELL, EVIDENTLY A LITTLE TIME IN BLACKGATE AND ARKHAM ASYLUM GAVE HIM REASON TO CHANGE SIDES.

GREAT.

ANYTHING ELSE?

GOTHAM POLICE

GOTHAM POLICE

POLICE

JUST GET HIM. HE'S HURTING PEOPLE.

YOU KNOW YOU CAN COUNT ON ME.

STEVE'S DINER

WELL, AT ANY RATE, SIR, I PREPARED YOU A LATE-NIGHT MEAL.

NO TIME, ALFRED. I'M ONLY HERE TO MAKE A FEW PREPARATIONS.

THE BEST PREPARATION IS A FULL STOMACH, MASTER BRUCE. IMAGINE IF YOUR STOMACH WERE TO GROWL AT THE WRONG TIME.

FINE.

AND WHAT ARE WE PREPARING FOR THIS EVENING?

GOT TO BE AN *AMBUSH*. I JUST NEED TO FIND OUT THE LOCATION.

INDEED. IT IS DIFFICULT TO BE AMBUSHED IF YOU ARE IN THE WRONG PLACE.

JUST LIKE I THOUGHT. THERE IS NO EATON PARK IN GOTHAM. MAYBE IT'S IN GOTHAM COUNTY.

BEGGING YOUR PARDON, SIR, BUT WHEN I FIRST ARRIVED IN GOTHAM I USED TO FREQUENT A SMALL DINER DOWN BY THE WATER. IT WAS CALLED EAT N PARK.

Chapter
Four

EAT N PARK

KRRSSHH

NOBODY MOVE!

DON'T WORRY, BATMANS. YOU'LL BE DOING ALL THE MOVING...

START DANCING, BATMAN!

FIRE!

RATTA-RATTA-RATTA!

UNGH!

RATTA-RATTA-RATTA!

ALL RIGHT, ALL RIGHT STOP SHOOTING. THERE AIN'T GONNA BE NOTHIN' LEFT OF HIM.

IS HE?

I DUNNO.

HE AIN'T MOVIN'.

LET'S GET A LOOK AT HIM BEFORE WE HAND HIM OVER.

IT'S STUCK. HE MUST'VE GLUED IT TO HIS FREAKIN' FACE.

WELL, IF THE MASK WON'T COME OFF...

...THEN LET'S TAKE OFF HIS WHOLE HEAD.

27

Chapter One

OKAY, OKAY! THAT'S ENOUGH FUN.

PUT THE BODY DOWN.

I'LL MAKE THE CALL.

YEAH. WE GOT HIM. AS A DOORNAIL. YEP. SO WHEN DO WE GET THE CASH?

Too soon.

One thing you can always rely on with criminals is that sooner or later they will do something stupid...

IT'S-IT'S NOT POSSIBLE--!

WILL YOU GUYS KEEP IT--

CLICK!

AHH!

GET AWAY!

NOOO!

STAY— STAY BACK!!

...which makes it impossible for me to always see a plan through to the end.

Even the best-laid plans call for improvisation.

YOU!

NO WAY THIS IS HAPPENING, MAAAN!

GIVE. ME. THAT. PHONE.

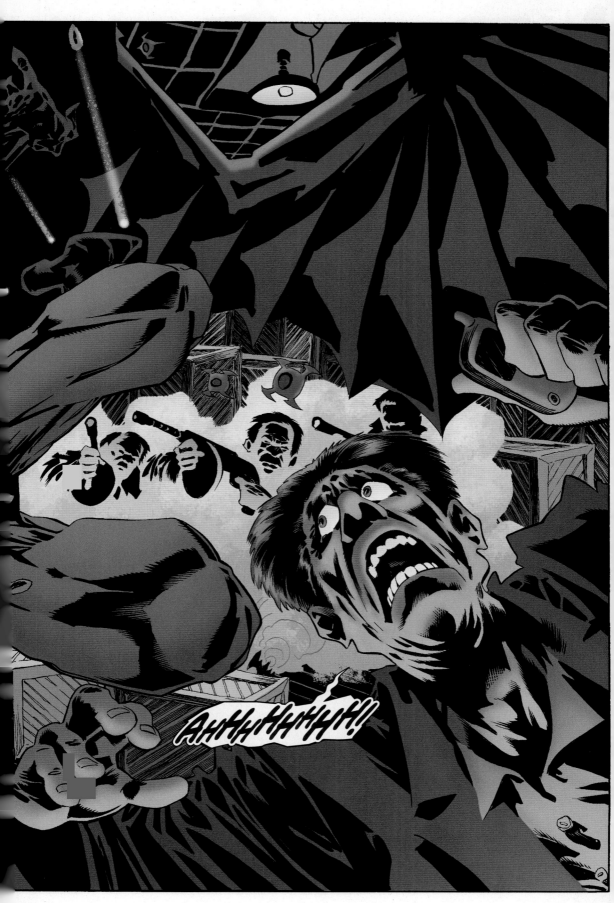

AGH!

Outgoing call Unknown.

WHO ARE YOU WORKING FOR? SCARECROW? IS *HE* YOUR BOSS?

WHO DID YOU CALL?

I DUNNO, MAN! IT WAS LEFT HERE FOR US!

Eye contact steady. He's telling the truth.

CLICK CLICK CLICK

CLICK

CLICK

CLICK CLICK

CLICK

CLICK

Like I said, improvise.

GET AWAY FROM FRANK!

LET HIM GO.

Deal with the situation at hand.

YOU HAVE SOMETHING ON YOUR SHIRTS.

HEY, HE'S RIGHT.

WHAT ARE THEY?

SOME KIND OF BURR--

BOOF!

BOOF! BOOF!

The big picture will eventually unfold.

I... MADE IT.

I GOT AWAY!

YOU FAILED TO DO AS I ASKED.

Y...YOU THE GUY ON THE PHONE? WE... WE TRIED, B...BUT BATMAN C...CAN'T BE KILLED. HE'S SOME KIND OF F... FREAK!

EVERYBODY DIES.

P...PLEASE...

I'M SORRY.

YOUR TIME IS UP.

THUTT

FOR NOW, YOU GO QUIETLY INTO THE NIGHT...

GOTHAM HISTORICAL SOCIETY

YOU'RE USUALLY FASTER THAN THIS, LANGSTROM.

SKREEEE!!

THE NAME'S *MAN-BAT*, AND I'VE BEEN WAITING FOR YOU, BATMAN.

Man-Bat's been using stealth to get the jump. Sitting and waiting isn't in his arsenal. This is another M.O. shake-up.

Just like Scarecrow.

I KNOW YOU CAN DO TWO THINGS AT ONCE, BATMAN.

NUH!

BUT EVEN BATMAN CAN'T HOLD TWO SARCOPHAGI *AND* COME AFTER ME.

DON'T DO IT, LANGSTROM! YOU'LL KILL THEM!

DTING!

TWACK

TWACK

TUNGG

AS TEMPTING AS IT IS TO RIP OUT YOUR THROAT RIGHT NOW...I CAN'T.

NUUUUH...WHO...ARE...YOU...WORKING...FOR?

I WORK FOR NO ONE!

S...SURE.

Close up, Man-Bat's eyes are cloudy.

He's not himself.

I SHOULD KILL YOU RIGHT HERE AND NOW!

Well, maybe a little.

But something is definitely off.

First Crane. Now Langstrom. I've got to find the connection.

If I survive tonight, that is.

SKSSSH!

OH MAN, WHAT HIT ME?

M...OVE.

AAAH!

NOW!!

OKAY!

I'M CLEAR!

CRASH!

COME ON! MOVE BEFORE BATS LOSES IT!

Chapter Three

YOU WIN. I'M GOING HOME. I NEED AT LEAST TWO HOURS OF SLEEP OR I'M WORTHLESS.

GOODNIGHT, BARRY.

CAN I HAVE A WORD?

BATMAN!

DETECTIVE CLARKSON. WE NEED TO *TALK.*

YOU WON'T NEED THAT.

SNAP!

I'M A COP, AND YOU'RE *SUPPOSED* TO BE A GOOD GUY, SO WHY WOULD YOU WORRY ABOUT MY GUN BEING OUT?

FINE.

FEEL BETTER?

MUCH.

WHAT DO YOU WANT?

EAT-N-PARK WAS MINE. I LEFT THE PACKAGE. THIS IS THE *THIRD* TIME YOU'VE TAKEN THE CREDIT.

GIVING YOU CREDIT WOULD BE CONDONING WHAT YOU DO, AND I WON'T DO THAT. PERIOD.

THEN YOU'RE LYING TO YOURSELF. YOU OWE THE PUBLIC THE *TRUTH.*

AREN'T *YOU* LYING EVERY TIME YOU PUT ON THAT COSTUME?

IT'S ABOUT THE MESSAGE. THE COSTUME. THE NEWS THAT I BROKE UP THEIR CRIME RING. THE NEWS AND THE RUMORS MAKE THINGS BETTER OUT THERE, MAKES THEM THINK *TWICE*.

IT KEEPS THE CRIMINALS LIVING UP IN *FEAR*.

YEAH, AND I SUPPOSE YOU HAVE HARD DATA TO SUPPORT YOUR CONCLUSION?

ACTUALLY I DO. I CAN HAVE A PRINTOUT SENT OVER TOMORROW.

I'M NOT GOING TO RETRACT MY REPORTS.

THEN THE *NEXT* ONE.

IT'S LATE. I HAVE WORK TO DO.

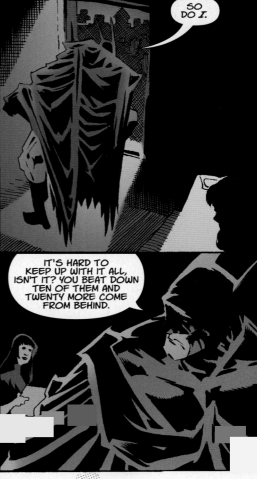

SO DO *I.*

IT'S HARD TO KEEP UP WITH IT ALL, ISN'T IT? YOU BEAT DOWN TEN OF THEM AND TWENTY MORE COME FROM BEHIND.

OH. MY.
GOD.

I've patrolled
this city most
of my life.

In that time, I've
learned to trust
my gut.

It's midnight in Gotham City and her citizens are running *scared*. They fear for their *lives*, and I fear that I may not be able to *help* them.

It started with the Scarecrow's escape from Arkham Asylum. He attempted to steal a *Hand of Glory*. That led me to the Axe-Man, who wanted to take my head as a souvenir. Then Man-Bat stole the mystical *Skull of Ra*. That's two supernatural artifacts and one ambush. It's all *wrong*.

And now there are rumors of a new threat. They say there is a *madman* loose on the streets. They say he takes his victims hearts... and *eats* them.

It's midnight in Gotham City and her citizens are running scared. Their city again sits on the precipice, dangerously close to descending into *madness*. It's my job to *stop* it.

Chapter One

VICHY CHAMPAGNE

IT'S TIME, MR. HEDGLEY...

YOU, EXPENSIVE AND CHEAP AT THE SAME TIME. MARVELOUS. PLEASE CLEAR THE AREA, MY DEAR. IT'S GOING TO GET MESSY, AND LUCKILY FOR YOU, IT IS NOT YOUR TIME.

SHIKT!

W...WHO ARE YOU?

WHO I AM IS OF LITTLE CONSEQUENCE AT THIS LATE HOUR.

WHAT AM I WOULD BE A QUESTION I AM PREPARED TO ANSWER. AND THE ANSWER IS...

...I AM YOUR KILLER!

SPLTCH

AAAHH!

A LITTLE DRAMATIC, DON'T YOU THINK?

HA. MAYBE I KNEW I HAD AN AUDIENCE. COME OUT AND SHOW YOURSELF.

ROOM SERVICE.

CLEVER, BUT A DEMONSTRATION OF YOUR TALENT'S ISN'T NECESSARY.

PLEASE. SHOW YOURSELF.

SO, HERE I AM.

GREETINGS, CLAYFACE.

WHAT DO YOU WANT? AND WHAT'S WITH THE ROBOT VOICE?

WE'RE A LOT ALIKE, YOU AND I.

YEAH? HOW YOU FIGURE?

BOTH TRAPPED INSIDE BODIES THAT MAKE THE WORLD HATE US.

MAYBE ME, BUT...

THIS IS THE REASON FOR THE ROBOT VOICE, AS YOU CALLED IT.

I'VE SEEN THE WONDERFUL THINGS YOU CAN DO, CLAYFACE, AND I BELIEVE, WITH A LITTLE WORK, YOU CAN DO EVEN MORE ASTOUNDING THINGS! YOU, MY FRIEND, CAN BE A GIANT!

I DON'T GET IT.

THE CITIZENS OF GOTHAM ARE BUT MERE FOOD FOR THE MIGHTY CONQUEROR WORM THAT IS CLAYFACE. THEY DO NOT STAND IN MY WAY. AND THEY MUST NOT STAND IN YOURS.

REMEMBER WHEN YOU BATTLED THE BATMAN AND ABSORBED HIM INTO YOU?

YEAH. HE BROKE OUT. IT HURT.

IT DOESN'T HAVE TO. YOU CAN USE THEM--YOU CAN USE HER--TO DESTROY THEM ALL.

REALLY?

FEAST. CONCENTRATE. SEE HOW MANY PEOPLE YOU CAN HOLD INSIDE OF YOU.

AND WHAT DO YOU DO YOU GET OUTTA THIS?

LESS ANTS FOR ME TO DEAL WITH.

BIGGER, YOU COULD CRUSH THE PEOPLE WHO POINT AND LAUGH. YOU COULD ABSORB THEM. THINK OF IT AS... RETURNING THEM TO THE EARTH!

YEAH... I LIKE THAT.

RETURN THEM TO THE EARTH.

O...OH... P...PLEASE... NO...

AAHHHHHHHHH!

DO YOU SEE? DO YOU SEE? CAN YOU FEEL THE POWER?!

OH YEAH.

GO! RETURN THEM ALL TO THE EARTH AND GROW TO THE HEIGHTS TO WHICH ONLY YOUR IMAGINATION CAN ASPIRE!

PERFECT.

PERFECT CHAOS!

LATER.

YOU DIDN'T NEED TO COME DOWN, COMMISSIONER.

I WAS ONLY SLEEPING FOR THE FIRST TIME IN 48 HOURS. WHY HASN'T THIS SCENE BEEN SECURED?

HEY, APRIL, YOU'RE NOT GOING TO BELIEVE THI--

NOT NOW, BARRY.

BUT...

WHAT YOUR PARTNER IS TRYING TO TELL YOU IS THAT WE HAVE *ANOTHER* CALL THAT MATCHES THIS.

TWO IN ONE NIGHT? WHERE'S THE NEW ONE?

GOTHAM RITZ HOTEL.

SO, WHAT DO WE KNOW ABOUT *THIS* MURDER?

THE BODY WAS FOUND TIED TO THE ARMS OF THE CLOCK. THE HEART WAS *MISSING.*

Chapter Two

WHAT CONNECTS THIS TO THE RITZ CRIME SCENE?

THE HEART WAS ALSO TAKEN.

GAH!

I KNOW ABOUT THE MURDER AT THE RITZ. I'VE ALREADY BEEN THERE. I CALLED THAT ONE IN TOO, DETECTIVE...

THE VICTIM WAS COUNCILMAN HEDGLEY.

HE'S ON THE BOARD OF DIRECTORS FOR BOTH ARKHAM AND GOTHAM GENERAL.

AND HE'S BEEN SKIMMING WHAT HE DIDN'T THINK WOULD BE NOTICED. TEN THOUSAND HERE, FIFTY THOUSAND THERE, ALL FROM THE POCKETS OF THE PATIENTS.

THAT DOESN'T MEAN THAT HE DESERVED TO DIE!

I FOUND THIS. I'LL BORROW IT FOR ANALYSIS.

I HAVE SOMEONE I NEED TO SPEAK WITH, GORDON. I'LL KEEP AN EYE ON THE SITUATION, BUT I SUGGEST YOU PUT EVERY AVAILABLE BODY ON THE STREETS. I BELIEVE THAT *CLAYFACE* IS INVOLVED, AND AT THIS POINT WE CAN ASSUME SOMETHING *BAD* IS GOING TO HAPPEN.

WE SHOULD BE *READY.*

UNBELIEVABLE.

CAN I SAY SOMETHING HERE? WHO DOES HE THINK HE IS? HE CAN'T JUST *TAKE* EVIDENCE! I THINK THE COMMISSIONER IS MORE THAN QUALIFIED TO MAKE ANY--

DETECTIVE CLARKSON?

YES?

HE'S ALREADY GONE.

CLARKSON, LUCAS, FINISH UP HERE AND THEN GET OVER TO THE HOTEL.

AND PLEASE, KEEP ME OUT OF YOUR SQUABBLES. I'M ONLY INTERESTED IN WHAT'S BEST FOR THE CITIZENS OF GOTHAM. AS YOU SHOULD BE.

RRRAAGHH!

OH MY GOD!

RUN!

OUTTA MY WAY!

YEEEESSS!

GOTHAM IS MIIIIINE!

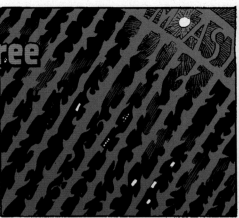

JONATHAN CRANE.

AHH! WHAT? WHO--WHO'S THERE?

YOU *KNOW* WHO IT IS, CRANE. ANSWER MY QUESTIONS AND I'LL BE OUT OF YOUR WAY.

W...WHAT'D I...I DO?

DON'T PLAY COY WITH ME. WHY DID YOU ATTEMPT TO STEAL A HAND OF GLORY?

STEAL? HAND OF WHO?

WHAT ARE THOSE MARKS?

I DON'T KNOW. HONEST. I WOKE UP AND I HAVE THESE HOLES AND THEY ITCH, MAN, AND THEN THEY TELL ME I BROKE IN SOME PLACE AND YOU SLAPPED ME AROUND AND I DON'T--

ENOUGH. I BELIEVE YOU.

REALLY?

HELLO? HELLOOOO?

AND THEY CALL ME CREEPY.

I KNOW SOMETHING YOU DON'T KNOW! I KNOW SOMETHING YOU DON'T KNOW!

CLANG!

HA HA HA HA HA HA HA HA

THE BATCAVE.

IT'S TOO MUCH.

I BEG YOUR PARDON, SIR?

SORRY, ALFRED, I DIDN'T REALIZE YOU WERE THERE. I WAS SAYING THERE'S TOO MUCH INFO, TOO MANY CLUES AND YET NONE OF THEM ADD UP OR POINT TO ANY OF THE USUAL SUSPECTS.

THAT'S AN ODD CONUNDRUM FOR YOU, SIR. THINGS DO SEEM ESPECIALLY *DARK* FOR GOTHAM THESE DAYS.

MOOD-ALTERING GAS AND MURDER USUALLY POINT TO THE JOKER, DON'T THEY SIR?

ONLY ONE PROBLEM WITH THAT THEORY: I JUST SAW THE JOKER LOCKED AWAY IN ARKHAM AN HOUR AGO.

I MAY HAVE TOO MANY *CLUES*.

BUT SHOCKINGLY FEW *FACTS*.

SCARECROW WAS CLEARLY NOT HIMSELF, BUT MAN-BAT SEEMED HIS USUAL FERAL SELF. EVEN SO, HE'S NOT THE TYPE TO ORGANIZE SOMETHING SO ELABORATE. HE'D JUST SHRED THE BODY, SO EVERYBODY KNEW HE WAS THE KILLER.

YET MAN-BAT IS CONNECTED BY THE ODD DECISION OF STEALING A SUPERNATURAL ARTIFACT LIKE SCARECROW.

BUT ONLY MAN-BAT ACTUALLY OBTAINED WHAT THEY SOUGHT.

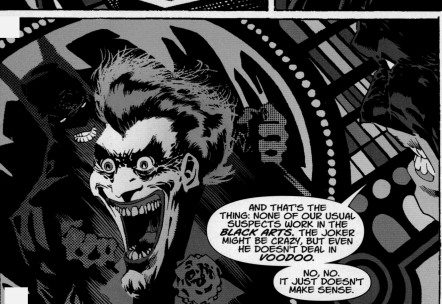

AND THAT'S THE THING: NONE OF OUR USUAL SUSPECTS WORK IN THE *BLACK ARTS*. THE JOKER MIGHT BE CRAZY, BUT EVEN HE DOESN'T DEAL IN *VOODOO*.

NO, NO. IT JUST DOESN'T MAKE SENSE.

AND THEN THERE IS THE GRUESOME FACT OF THE HEARTS BEING REMOVED FROM THE TWO VICTIMS.

I THINK THERE IS A DISTINCT POSSIBILITY YOU HAVE A NEW PLAYER IN GOTHAM.

MAYBE, OR AN OLD ONE TRYING TO THROW ME OFF. LET'S NOT FORGET THAT ONE VICTIM WAS A COMMON THUG AND THE OTHER A HIGH-RANKING, ALBEIT CORRUPT, OFFICIAL.

I'M GOING TO REST FOR 15 MINUTES BEFORE I START MY PRE-SUNRISE ROUNDS. I'M STILL FEELING THE AFTEREFFECTS OF THAT KNOCKOUT PILL I TOOK AT EAT-N-PARK.

YES, GETTING SHOT AND PRETENDING TO BE DEAD CAN TAKE A LOT OUT OF A MAN.

WAKE ME IF ANYTHING--

--COMES UP.

SOMETHING JUST HAS, MASTER BRUCE.

IT APPEARS COMMISSIONER GORDAN HAS ACTIVATED THE BAT-SIGNAL.

I'LL MAKE SURE THE BATMOBILE IS REFUELED.

DON'T BOTHER.

I'M GOING TO NEED SOMETHING *BIGGER*.

74

DO YOU HEAR ME, GOTHAM? THERE IS NO ESCAPING CLAYFACE!

BRILLIANT. PERFECT CHAOS HAS LED TO PERFECT FEAR.

GUESS WHO?

STAY BACK!

NO!

AAAHHH!

IT IS TIME FOR ME TO BE... ELSEWHERE.

PUNY HUMANS-- YOU CAN RUN, BUT YOU CAN'T HIDE!

CLAYFACE!

COME ON!

FIGHTING CLAYFACE MAN-TO-MAN IS USUALLY ILL-ADVISED, SIR. MIGHT I SUGGEST EXPOSING THE BEAST TO A LARGE BODY OF WATER?

IF I CAN'T BEAT HIM, HOW CAN I DRAG HIM TO THE WATER?

AH YES. GOOD POINT.

SLAM!

AHHHH!

GOT HIM!

BATMAN, THE BUILDING BEHIND YOU IS STILL FULL OF PEOPLE.

CAN'T HOLD HIM LONG...

I NEED YOU TO TELL ME WHAT BUILDINGS ARE UNOCCUPIED... AND OWNED BY WAYNE.

VERY GOOD, SIR. VERY GOOD INDEED.

RRRAAGHH!

THE CLOSEST WAYNE-OWNED BUILDING IS 180 DEGREES DIRECTLY BEHIND YOU.

THANK YOU.

CRASH!

THAT WAS FUN. NOW I GET TO THROW YOU AROUND!

UNGH!

WHAM!

SIR, ARE YOU ALL RIGHT?

I'M DOWN, BUT DON'T WORRY. IT WAS DESIGNED FOR THIS.

YOU'RE NOT THE ONLY ONE WHO CAN GROW.

JUUUP!

WHOA.

AHHH!

ARGH!

AAAH!

UNGH!

OH NO!

UNGH!

BATMAN, WHAT'S GOING ON?

AHHH!

ARGH!

THE PEOPLE INSIDE CLAYFACE ARE STILL *ALIVE!*

I'LL HAVE TO GO FOR THE HEAD.

THERE'S A LARGE APARTMENT BUILDING THAT IS VACATED ON THE NORTHEAST CORNER. WAYNE ALSO OWNS IT.

STOP WHILE YOU CAN, CLAYFACE. YOU ARE HARMING INNOCENT CITIZENS. *SURRENDER.*

NOBODY IS INNOCENT IN GOTHAM AND I *NEVER* SURRENDER! YOU HEAR ME, BAT--

MRLPH!

SPLTCH!

ALL RIGHT, BATMAN. LET'S *RUMBLE.*

Chapter
Two

STARGAZING, THE BIRD WATCHING OF THE URBAN RETIRED.

WHAT THE HECK?

BUT TONIGHT, MORE THAN JUST CONSTELLATIONS FILL THE GOTHAM SKY.

LET'S JUST SEE WHAT WE HAVE HERE.

GIANT ROBOT FIGHTING A GIANT MONSTER? FIGURES.

SPLTCH!

THUMP!

ZZZIP!

TOO EASY. SOOOO EASY.

AND NOW, TO THE BALL!

Chapter Three

KKRRSSSHH!

YOU'VE GOT TO STOP, CLAYFACE. THE PEOPLE INSIDE YOU ARE STILL ALIVE, AND THEY'RE GETTING HURT.

DON'T WORRY, BATMAN. I'M FEEDING THEM AIR. THAT'S THE THING ABOUT CLAY AND MUD, IT BREATHES.

ALFRED, RELAY AN UNTRACEABLE MESSAGE TO GORDON.

Chapter Four

WHEN THE BELLS DIDN'T RING AT MIDNIGHT, THE MONSIGNOR GOT WORRIED, SO HE WENT UP TO CHECK.

WE GOT THE CALL A MINUTE LATER. THE VICTIM'S HEART IS MISSING. JUST LIKE THE OTHERS.

FREDRICK FRANCIS CATHEDRAL

HAZEL COURT

VAN ARK. DAMN. HE WAS ON THE JOB.

NOT EVEN THE *CHURCH* IS SAFE IN GOTHAM ANYMORE...

BRAY FOUNDRY 1956

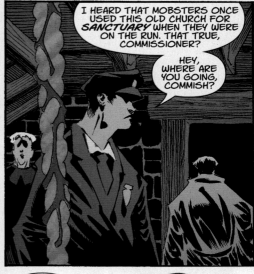

I HEARD THAT MOBSTERS ONCE USED THIS OLD CHURCH FOR *SANCTUARY* WHEN THEY WERE ON THE RUN. THAT TRUE, COMMISSIONER?

HEY, WHERE ARE YOU GOING, COMMISH?

I'VE GOT TO MAKE A TELEPHONE CALL.

LATER.

I've always found confusion to be the best tool against thugs like Clayface.

Clayface is many things, but smart is not one of them.

YOU JUST RECEIVED AN ENCRYPTED MESSAGE FROM COMMISSIONER GORDON, SIR. HE WOULD LIKE YOU TO MEET HIM AT GOTHAM CEMETERY.

CEMETERY? STRANGE.

I'M ON MY WAY, ALFRED. HAVE ARRANGEMENTS BEEN MADE FOR SATURDAY NIGHT'S GALA BENEFIT BALL FOR THE RECONSTRUCTION OF THE ARBORETUM?

ALL IS IN HAND, SIR.

WHY THE SECRECY, JIM?

YOU CAUSED SOME MAJOR DAMAGE TONIGHT. THE GOVERNOR AND THE MAYOR ARE ON THE RAMPAGE. THEY WANT YOUR HEAD.

HOW MANY CIVILIAN FATALITIES?

NONE.

IF THE MAYOR AND GOVERNOR HAD GOTHAM'S BEST INTERESTS AT HEART, *THAT'S* WHAT THEY'D BE WORRIED ABOUT.

THE DAMAGE WILL BE TAKEN CARE OF. I'VE ALREADY HEARD WAYNE IS THROWING A FUNDRAISER FOR HIS LOSSES, AND SO IS DUNKIRK. THE BUILDINGS CAN BE REPAIRED, PEOPLE CAN'T. I PUT LIVES AHEAD OF PROPERTY. THAT WAS MY CALL. TELL THE SUITS THEY CAN TAKE IT UP WITH ME IF THEY DON'T LIKE IT.

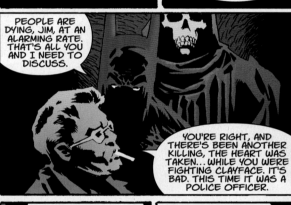

PEOPLE ARE DYING, JIM, AT AN ALARMING RATE. THAT'S ALL YOU AND I NEED TO DISCUSS.

YOU'RE RIGHT, AND THERE'S BEEN ANOTHER KILLING, THE HEART WAS TAKEN... WHILE YOU WERE FIGHTING CLAYFACE. IT'S BAD. THIS TIME IT WAS A POLICE OFFICER.

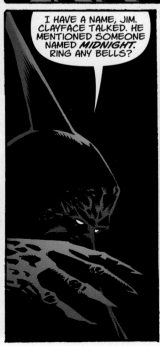

I HAVE A NAME, JIM. CLAYFACE TALKED. HE MENTIONED SOMEONE NAMED *MIDNIGHT*. RING ANY BELLS?

THIS BLOWS OUR PATTERN TO BITS. THE OTHERS WERE CRIMINALS, CORRUPT. NOW THE ONLY CONNECTION IS THE HEART REMOVAL.

THAT MAY NOT BE ENTIRELY TRUE, BATMAN.

THE VICTIM WAS CAPTAIN DOUGLAS VAN ARK. HE RETIRED EARLY AFTER HIS NAME SHOWED UP IN THE BOOKS FOR SEVERAL MOBSTERS INCLUDING THE PENGUIN AND THE JOKER.

SO WE HAVE A NAME AND POSSIBLE MOTIVATION. THIS MIDNIGHT IS SEEKING REVENGE ON CRIMINALS AND TAKING THEIR HEARTS AS SOUVENIRS. FOR WHAT MORBID REASON IS ANYBODY'S GUESS.

TAKE AWAY MURDER AND IT COULD BE YOU.

THAT'S A BIG THING TO TAKE AWAY. WHOEVER MIDNIGHT IS, HE IS CLEARLY PSYCHOTIC AND NEEDS TO BE BROUGHT IN.

I ALSO BELIEVE MIDNIGHT HAD SOMETHING TO DO WITH SCARECROW AND CLAYFACE'S CRIMES. CLAYFACE SPOKE ABOUT MIDNIGHT LIKE A FRIEND WHO LET HIM DOWN, AND SCARECROW WAS DRUGGED. HE HAS NO RECOLLECTION OF OUR ENCOUNTER.

AND MAN-BAT?

HE HAD EVERY CHANCE IN THE WORLD TO KILL ME, AND DIDN'T. DOES THAT SOUND LIKE MAN-BAT? IN FACT, THEY'VE ALL HAD A COUPLE OPEN SHOTS AT ME AND LET ME GO.

SO MIDNIGHT WANTS YOU ALIVE?

MAYBE THE SHOW IS FOR ME?

YOU SAID IT YOURSELF: TAKE AWAY THE KILLING AND MIDNIGHT SOUNDS LIKE ME. MAYBE THIS IS ANOTHER PSYCHO WHO THINKS HE'S A CRIME FIGHTER.

MAYBE IT'S... NO. CURSE ME FOR EVEN THINKING IT.

THAT KILLING THE SCUM IS EASIER? OF COURSE IT IS.

IT'S NOTHING TO TAKE A LIFE AND EVERYTHING TO SAVE ONE, JIM.

Chapter Five

MR. WAYNE, ARE YOU HAVING A FUNDRAISER BECAUSE YOU'RE BROKE?

OF COURSE NOT. I HAVE ALREADY PLEDGED TO EQUAL *EVERY* SINGLE DONATION MADE THIS EVENING.

HELLO, EVERYBODY! LET'S GET THIS THING STARTED, SHALL WE?

HEY, CAREFUL THERE, HENDERSON. YOU'RE ON DUTY, AREN'T YOU?

JUST PARTY DUTY, SIR. ≥HIC!≤

HAVING A GOOD NIGHT, COMMISSIONER? MAYOR?

GREAT. THANKS.

LIEUTENANT CLARKSON! I DON'T BELIEVE I'VE EVER SEEN YOU IN A DRESS. YOU LOOK LOVELY.

RAVISHING.

THANK YOU. YOU HAVE ANY IDEA HOW HARD IT IS TO FIT A GLOCK INSIDE ONE OF THESE LITTLE PURSES?

EXCUSE ME, LADIES.

MAYOR, COMMISSIONER GORDON, I THINK YOU ALL KNOW *RICHARD DUNKIRK*. HE'S TOO MODEST TO SAY IT, BUT HE IS *DOUBLING* EVERY DONATION MADE TONIGHT.

OH, UM, LIEUTENANT CLARKSON, HAVE YOU MET OUR HOST, MR. BRUCE WAYNE?

PLEASED TO MEET YOU, MISS CLARKSON.

LIEUTENANT... AND THANK YOU FOR A LOVELY EVENING.

HOW ABOUT NOT HITTING ON MY LADY RIGHT IN FRONT OF ME, WAYNE. I DON'T CARE WHO YOU ARE. I'LL POP YOU ONE.

CALM DOWN, RICHARD. YOUR INHERITANCE IS SHOWING.

YOUR LADY?!

I'M FLATTERED, MR. WAYNE. AND MR. DUMKIRK, I PREFER MY BILLIONAIRES WITH A LITTLE MORE INTELLIGENCE.

SMOOTH MOVE, RICH.

THE SASHIMI IS AS FRESH AS IT COMES. I ALSO RECOMMEND THE MUSHROOM CAPS STUFFED WITH CRAB.

QUITE A SPREAD. THIS HOW YOU EAT EVERY NIGHT?

NO. USUALLY I HAVE IT DELIVERED.

I HAVE TO ASK BECAUSE I'VE KNOWN HIM SINCE HE TORTURED BUGS WITH A TIFFANY'S MAGNIFYING GLASS. DUNKIRK?

IT'S A BLIND DATE. GOD, I DON'T EVEN KNOW WHY I'M TELLING YOU THIS.

AND DON'T WORRY BECAUSE HE STOPPED TORTURING BUGS LAST WEEK. NEXT WEEK HE GETS HIS GOLD-ENCRUSTED BIG BOY PANTS.

HAHA!

I HAVE TO SAY, MI...LIEUTENANT CLARKSON, I'M A BIT INTIMIDATED. YOUR FATHER WAS A LEGEND. MY FATHER USED TO SAY HE WAS THE ELIOT NESS OF GOTHAM.

THANK YOU. HE CAST QUITE THE LONG SHADOW.

I THINK I KNOW SOMETHING ABOUT THAT.

CRASH!

H...HEARTS...
-<CLICK>--...
WHIRRRR...H...
H...HEART'S...

SKREEEE!

WHAT'S THAT SOUND?

WHAT'S GOING ON?!?

SMASH!

SKREEEE!

MMMIDNIGHHHT--

--YOU BETRAAAAAYED ME!

SSSKRIPP!

SSSKRIPP!

HELP!

IF YOU'LL EXCUSE ME, DETECTIVE, I, UM, MUST BE GOING--

STAY BACK, WAYNE!

AAAHHH!!

LOOK OUT!

RUN!

ALL OF YOU ARE LIARS!

SKREEEEE!

WAYNE, GET OUT OF MY WAY!

WHAT ARE YOU DOING?!

GETTING OUT OF THE WAY!

DON'T MOVE! GET DOWN ON THE GROUND OR WE'LL BE FORCED TO FIRE!

Hold steady, Miss Clarkson. I only have one dart in this cufflink.

PFFT!

Chapter Two

WHAT HAPPENED?

HE COLLAPSED.

HE COULD BE FAKING. PROCEED WITH CAUTION.

GOOD HEAVENS! DO YOU THINK HE'S *DEAD?*

GET OFF ME... COWARD.

SMOOTH MOVE, WAYNE.

SHUT UP, DUNKIRK.

REMOVE THE MASK. LET'S SEE WHO THIS "MIDNIGHT" CHARACTER IS.

MY GOD...

SERGEANT HENDERSON!

BUT I SAW HIM WHEN I CAME IN THIS EVENING.

MIDNIGHT IS A *POLICE OFFICER?*

THIS IS OBVIOUSLY A RUSE. THIS IS ALSO POLICE BUSINESS, WAYNE, SO IF YOU DON'T MIND...

HE HAS A PULSE! HE'S STILL ALIVE, BUT HE'S LOSING A LOT OF BLOOD.

PARAMEDICS ARE ON THE WAY.

STRAP HIM DOWN TIGHTLY, FELLAS.

HE'S NOT GOING TO MAKE IT IF THEY DON'T--

WAYNE -- WHAT ARE YOU DOING?

APPLY PRESSURE HERE, LIEUTENANT.

107

IMPRESSIVE, WAYNE. I DIDN'T KNOW YOU COULD *BUY* A MEDICAL LICENSE.

MY FATHER WAS A DOCTOR. I PICKED UP A FEW THINGS.

NOW IF YOU'LL EXCUSE ME, LIEUTENANT, I HAVE A BIG MESS TO HAVE CLEANED UP.

IF HENDERSON EVER WAKES UP, WE CAN ONLY HOPE HE KNOWS SOMETHING ABOUT WHO DID THIS TO HIM... AND WHY.

DO YOU THINK THERE'S ANY CHANCE HENDERSON AND MIDNIGHT ARE--

ABSOLUTELY NOT. HENDERSON DROVE WITH ME HERE TONIGHT. WHATEVER HAPPENED OCCURRED AFTER WE ARRIVED.

HOW WAS THE CHARITY BALL, SIR? I COULDN'T HELP BUT NOTICE MOST OF THE GUESTS FLED *SCREAMING*.

NOT NOW, ALFRED.

I NEED TO GET BACK TO THE MANOR RIGHT AWAY.

LATER, IN THE BATCAVE...

I need to get to Langstrom before his memories fade, and before the doctors at Arkham Asylum get their hands on him. I need him to tell me what he knows about Midnight.

I HAVE TEA AND FINGER SANDWICHES, MASTER BRUCE.

SIGH.

DO WE NEED TO TALK, SIR?

TALK?

WHAT DO WE NEED TO TALK ABOUT?

I THINK I MAY HAVE CROSSED A LINE... WHEN I COMMENTED ON YOUR ACTIONS AT THE CHARITY BALL.

NO NEED TO TALK, ALFRED...

...BECAUSE YOU WERE RIGHT.

HE'S PREPPED. WE'LL BEGIN THE TREATMENT AS SOON AS DR. LAJOS ARRIVES. PAGE ME.

SO... YOU THINK THOSE CHAINS WILL HOLD HIM?

YEAH, HE'S SEDATED. STILL, THEY DON'T PAY ME ENOUGH TO GO IN THERE. DO YOU KNOW WHAT HAPPENS IN THAT ROOM? *ELECTROSHOCK TREATMENTS.* THE DOC PUTS THEM ELECTRODES ON THEIR SKULLS, TURNS ON THE JUICE, AND THEY START THRASHING AND SCREAMING.

THAT'S WHY THEY *SOUNDPROOF* THE ROOMS. SO THE OTHER PATIENTS WON'T KNOW *WHAT* GOES ON IN THERE.

I LIKED IT BETTER WHEN *I* DIDN'T KNOW WHAT WENT ON IN THERE.

WAKE UP, LANGSTROM. YOUR LIFE IS IN *DANGER,* AND WE NEED TO *TALK.*

I *KNOW* YOU'RE AWAKE. YOU CAN'T *FOOL ME.*

WE DON'T HAVE MUCH TIME. THEY'RE COMING TO ELECTROCUTE YOU--TO TURN YOU INTO A *VEGETABLE*--AND I NEED YOUR BRAIN *FUNCTIONING.* I NEED *KIRK LANGSTROM.*

LOOSEN THE STRAPS.

DO I NEED TO *FORCE* YOU TO DRINK THIS?

NEXT TIME I WON'T GO SO EASY.

OF COURSE YOU WON'T.

BATMAN. HOW DID I GET HERE?

YOU'RE GOING TO BE ALL RIGHT, KIRK. I NEED YOU TO TELL ME ABOUT *MIDNIGHT.*

IT'S HAZY. I CAN'T ALWAYS RECALL EVERYTHING I DO AS MAN-BAT. I REMEMBER MIDNIGHT APPROACHING ME TO FORM SOME SORT OF ALLIANCE.

BUT YOU WERE BETRAYED?

HE SLIPPED ME SOME KIND OF DRUG... MADE ME DO THINGS.

I NEED A LOCATION, KIRK. A NAME. ANYTHING I CAN USE TO TRACK DOWN MIDNIGHT.

DUNKIRK TOWER. I MET MIDNIGHT TWICE ON THE ROOF OF DUNKIRK TOWER.

THEY'RE-- THEY'RE COMING IN!

THANK YOU, KIRK.

WHAT IS THIS? WHERE IS THE MONSTER!?!

HE'LL BE BACK SOON ENOUGH. DON'T YOU WORRY.

DUNKIRK
TOWER.

THE
FOLLOWING
NIGHT.

11:55 P.M.

DUNKIRK
INDUSTRIES

WE ♥ GOTHAM

Chapter Four

LIAR

KILLER

AH, RIGHT ON TIME.

I'LL BE WITH YOU IN A MOMENT, BATMAN. I JUST WANT TO GET MY JARS IN ORDER.

NO. YOU HAVE ONE CHANCE. STAY OUT OF MY WAY, OR YOU AND YOUR CITY WILL TRULY LEARN WHAT IT MEANS TO LIVE IN FEAR.

ONE CHANCE: SURRENDER. NOW.

BRILLIANT. I ASSUME YOU ARE READY FOR OUR FIRST FIGHT, THEN?

OR SHOULD I SAY, OUR LAST!

THWAP!

THWAP!

BOOOOM!

119

Meanwhile...

WHERE IS HE? TOO LATE FOR BUSINESS ANYWAY. I SHOULD HAVE KNOWN IT WAS A PRANK.

OR MAYBE NOT. HMMMM.

MR. BLAGUEUR?

I PREFER MONSIEUR BLAGUEUR.

RIGHT THIS WAY, *MONSIEUR BLAGUEUR.* I THINK YOU WILL FIND THE HOUSE VERY MUCH TO YOUR LIKING.

IT'S QUITE THE FIXER-UPPER, ISN'T IT?

NOTHING A SPOT OF PAINT CAN'T COVER!

RIGHT THIS WAY. MIND THE PORCH. THE BOARDS ARE LOOSE.

THAT'S ONE WAY TO DISPOSE OF UNWANTED TRICK-OR-TREATERS.

UM, YES, HEH. THIS WAY, PLEASE.

VOILÀ! YOU SIMPLY WILL NOT FIND A PIECE OF PROPERTY LIKE THIS IN GOTHAM FOR THE PRICE I'M SELLING. IT'S A ONCE IN A LIFETIME OPPORTUNITY.

VERY IMPRESSIVE. WHAT CAN I SAY? I'M FEELING IMPULSIVE...

I'LL TAKE IT!

HEH, HEH. YOU REALLY STARTLED ME THERE FOR A SECOND.

THE STUPID THING IS JAMMED.

BANG.

BANG!

THIS IS GOING TO BE THE BEST HALLOWEEN EVER!

HA HA HA HA HA HA

HAPPY HALLOWEEN

NEXT:
TRICK OR TREAT!

...IF YOU DARE...

THANK YOU FOR JOINING ME FOR BRUNCH, APRIL.

I ALREADY ATE BREAKFAST, SO THIS IS LUNCH... I ONLY HAVE AN HOUR, BRUCE.

BIG HALLOWEEN NIGHT PLANS?

FOR COPS IT'S ALWAYS A BIG NIGHT. PLUS THIS YEAR WE HAVE A FULL MOON *AND* THAT MIDNIGHT CHARACTER ON THE LOOSE, WHICH MEANS THAT *ALL* THE CRAZIES WILL BE IN TOP FORM.

Chapter One

WELL, I'M GLAD YOU TOOK THE TIME TO MEET WITH ME. I FELT TERRIBLE ABOUT WHAT HAPPENED AT THE GALA, AND EVEN THOUGH HE DESERVES IT, I SHOULD NOT HAVE "HIT" ON YOU IN FRONT OF DUNKIRK.

REALLY? THAT WAS THE ONE THING YOU DID I *DIDN'T* MIND. I'D RATHER BE SINGLE THE REST OF MY LIFE THAN DATE A SPOILED ROTTEN BRAT.

THEN WHY DID YOU ACCEPT MY INVITATION?

PLAYING THE ODDS, I GUESS. EVERY BILLIONAIRE IN GOTHAM CAN'T BE A LOSER, RIGHT?

SERIOUSLY THOUGH, HOW COME SUCH A LOVELY, STRONG WOMAN IS STILL SINGLE?

IT'S MORE ME THAN THEM. I'M MARRIED TO THE JOB. THE ONLY PROBLEM IS THAT I WON'T DATE ANOTHER COP, SO YOU CAN SEE THE VICIOUS CIRCLE.

I DO INDEED. I HAVE THE SAME PROBLEM MYSELF.

SEEMS TO ME YOU'RE OUT WITH A NEW SUPERMODEL EVERY WEEKEND.

EXACTLY. NEVER THE SAME ONE, JUST AN ENDLESS REVOLVING DOOR OF PRETTY FACES.

YOU POOR MAN.

I HOPE YOU WON'T THINK ME TOO FORWARD, BUT I BOUGHT YOU A TRINKET AS AN APOLOGY FOR MY BEHAVIOR.

ARE THOSE REAL? BRUCE, I REALLY DON'T--

APRIL, PLEASE.

BRUCE, THIS IS FAR TOO EXTRAVAGANT. I REALLY CAN'T--

OH!

SNAP!

CLEARLY MONEY IS THE MOST IMPORTANT THING IN YOUR LIFE, MR. WAYNE. YOU SHOWER YOUR MODELS WITH GIFTS, AND I'M SURE THEY GIVE YOU WHAT YOU WANT IN EXCHANGE.

BUT I....

Chapter Two

AFTER MUCH DELIBERATION, THE ONLY CONCLUSION I CAN MAKE AT THIS TIME...

...IS THAT I HAVE *NO* CLUE WHAT IS HAPPENING IN GOTHAM, *WHO* MIDNIGHT IS, OR *WHAT* HE REALLY WANTS. I HAVE NOTHING.

CLICK

NOTHING!

SKREE!

SKREE!

SKREE!

SKREE!

SKREE!

BEGGING YOUR PARDON, SIR, BUT IF NOT NOW, THEN WHEN? YOU HAVE A UNIQUE ABILITY TO AVOID WHAT YOU CHOOSE TO AVOID.

AND LET'S NOT FORGET WHAT HAPPENED LAST TIME YOU LET SOMETHING BOTTLE UP.

IS SOMETHING BESIDES TODAY'S BRUNCH FIASCO UPSETTING YOU, MASTER BRUCE?

NOT NOW, ALFRED.

MY PERSONAL LIFE DOESN'T EXIST WHEN I WEAR THIS COWL. RIGHT NOW I WANT TO CRACK THIS MIDNIGHT CASE BEFORE MORE PEOPLE DIE.

ALL OF THE VICTIMS HAVE BEEN CRIMINALS, MORE OR LESS, SO WHAT DOES THAT HAVE TO DO WITH THESE ARCANE ARTIFACTS? THEY JUST DON'T CONNECT.

UNLESS--OF COURSE!--THEY AREN'T *SUPPOSED* TO CONNECT. WHAT IF MIDNIGHT'S PLAN WAS SO UTTERLY SIMPLE THAT HE CHOSE THESE DISTRACTIONS JUST TO KEEP ME GUESSING?

I'M NO DETECTIVE, SIR, BUT THAT DOES SOUND INTERESTING...

UNFORTUNATELY DUTY CALLS...IT'S THE BAT-SIGNAL, SIR.

Chapter Three

I THOUGHT THINGS WERE TOO HOT FOR ME TO COME HERE?

STILL ARE. LET'S MAKE THIS QUICK.

TWO ENVELOPES WERE FOUND IN THIS DEAD BUS DRIVER'S HANDS. NOW THERE'S ONLY ONE.

AND IT HAS MY NAME ON IT.

LOOKS OKAY.

BATMAN,
I HAVE A BUSLOAD OF KIDDIES DRESSED UP AS GHOSTS AND GHOULS. COME TO MY PARTY OR I'LL MAKE THEM GHOSTS FOR REAL. HAPPY HALLOWEEN!
XOXO.

JOKER

I enjoy Halloween not for the reasons most citizens of Gotham do...

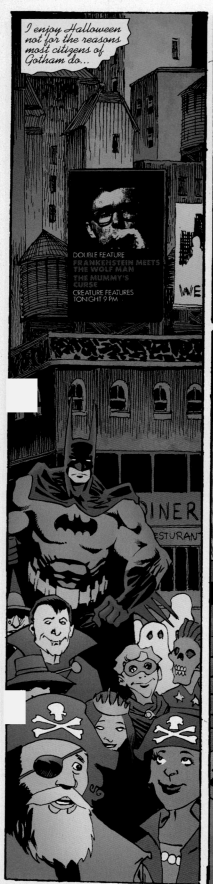

...but because for me, this is the closest Batman can get to the general populace without there being life-threatening emergencies.

There's not much to enjoy tonight, though.

DOUBLE FEATURE
FRANKENSTEIN MEETS THE WOLF MAN
THE MUMMY'S CURSE
CREATURE FEATURES
TONIGHT 9 PM.

WE

DINER
RESTAURANT

NICE UTILITY BELT, DUDE!

THANK YOU.

The Joker has escaped and kidnapped children, and Midnight's murder spree seems to grow by the night.

As much as I'd like to move among the citizens, tonight it is just not to be.

Tonight it's too dangerous. Too unpredictable.

BRUCE.

OLIVER.

Anybody could be hiding in this crowd.

The margin for error is too great...

LET'S GO, FREEZE, IT'S TIME FOR BOB WILKINS'S CREATURE FEATURES...

NO PARKING

NOW PLAYING HOUSE ON HAUNTED HI

COME ON, CARTER, YOU HAVE *ENOUGH* CANDY!

DON'T SAY THOSE WORDS TO ME!

...and I have a party to attend.

This way... he's <u>close</u>.

There it is--<u>his home</u>.

From here I can spot four traps.

The windows are wired, most likely with explosives.

The stairs have been cut to break when stepped on.

There are wires running between the railings attached to a spring-action projectile.

HAPPY HALLOWEEN

Assuming I stepped around all the obvious traps, that leaves the biggest for the front door.

It's almost *too* obvious...

...but that doorknob looks like it was recently installed.

I'll start there.

POP!!

BOOOM!!

YOU KNOW, YOU COULD HAVE KNOCKED.

WHERE ARE THE KIDS, JOKER?

THAT *IS* THE QUESTION OF THE NIGHT, ISN'T IT? JUST WHERE *ARE* THOSE DARN KIDS?

THIS IS THE LAST TIME I ASK.

WHERE. ARE. THE. KIDS?

YOU HARDLY HAVE THE UPPER HAND HERE, BATBOY. IF YOU HURT ME I MIGHT FORGET WHERE THEY ARE, AND THEN THOSE POOR LITTLE DEARS WOULD SLOWLY STARVE TO DEATH. DO YOU THINK CHILDREN WOULD RESORT TO *CANNIBALISM* TO SURVIVE? PERSONALLY, I DON'T THINK ONLY ADULTS ARE CORRUPT ENOUGH TO CONSIDER EATING UNCLE GEORGE TO SURVIVE. BUT WHAT ARE *YOUR* THOUGHTS ON THE TOPIC?

KRAKK!

I ALREADY ASKED FOR THE LAST TIME. SHALL WE CONTINUE?

W...WAIT. I HAVE SOMETHING TO ADD...

WHACK! THOK!

WE MAKE AN EXCELLENT TEAM. PERHAPS YOU WOULD LIKE TO STAND BY MY SIDE ON A MORE PERMANENT BASIS?

HA. HA. HA. HEE. HEE.

MY OFFER IS FUNNY TO YOU?

WELL, *EVERYTHING* IS FUNNY TO ME, BUT THAT IS *HYSTERICAL!* YOU WANT *ME* TO STAND BY *YOU?* PLEASE, I RUN THIS TOWN AND BATS IS MY TOY, YOU GOT THAT, NIGHTY-NIGHT?

THAT'S A SHAME. I THOUGHT WE SAW EYE TO EYE.

YOUR ONLY MISTAKE WAS THINKING I WOULD WORK FOR YOU WHEN CLEARLY IT IS *YOU* WHO SHOULD WORK FOR *ME!*

TAKE YOUR DIGIT OFF ME.

ENOUGH!

KRAK!

KONGG!

I'LL DEAL WITH MIDNIGHT LATER. FIRST, WE NEED TO *TALK.*

Never fails. Put two megalomaniacal villains in a room together and inevitably they'll tear each other apart.

Now it's my turn.

WHERE ARE THEY, JOKER?

I'LL GIVE YOU A HINT... I WAS KIDDING ABOUT THEIR STARVING. BUT IF YOU REALLY WANT A TASTY TIDBIT, HOW ABOUT YOU-KNOW-WHO'S TRUE IDENTITY?

WHAT?

Chapter Five

THEY'RE SCARED BUT THEY'LL BE OKAY. TOO BAD YOUR *FRIEND* HAD TO SAVE THAT PSYCHOPATHIC FREAK TO FIND OUT WHERE THEY WERE.

THAT'S NOT ALL I FOUND OUT, LIEUTENANT.

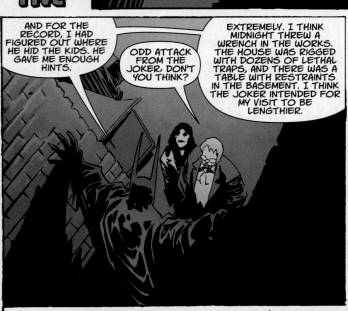

AND FOR THE RECORD, I HAD FIGURED OUT WHERE HE HID THE KIDS. HE GAVE ME ENOUGH HINTS.

ODD ATTACK FROM THE JOKER, DON'T YOU THINK?

EXTREMELY. I THINK MIDNIGHT THREW A WRENCH IN THE WORKS. THE HOUSE WAS RIGGED WITH DOZENS OF LETHAL TRAPS, AND THERE WAS A TABLE WITH RESTRAINTS IN THE BASEMENT. I THINK THE JOKER INTENDED FOR MY VISIT TO BE LENGTHIER.

DIDN'T YOU SAY YOU GOT SOMETHING ELSE OUT OF THE JOKER?

YES.

HE TOLD ME MIDNIGHT'S TRUE IDENTITY.

HE SAID IT WAS *BARRY LUCAS*...YOUR *PARTNER*, LIEUTENANT CLARKSON.

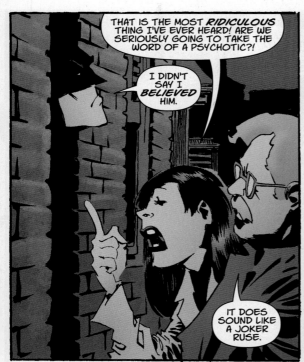

THAT IS THE MOST *RIDICULOUS* THING I'VE EVER HEARD! ARE WE SERIOUSLY GOING TO TAKE THE WORD OF A PSYCHOTIC?!

I DIDN'T SAY I *BELIEVED* HIM.

IT DOES SOUND LIKE A JOKER RUSE.

BUT I AM WONDERING WHERE OFFICER LUCAS IS RIGHT NOW...

Meanwhile....

LATE AGAIN AND NOW THIS. CLARKSON AND GORDON ARE GOING TO HAVE MY HIDE.

I CAN'T CATCH A BREAK.

BETTER CALL IN AND LET THEM KNOW.

CAN'T CATCH A BREAK, BUDDY?

It's midnight in Gotham City and a police detective is missing.

YOU CAN SIT THIS ONE OUT IF YOU WANT, DETECTIVE.

THANKS, SIR, BUT I'D RATHER STAY ON AND STAY CLOSE IF THAT'S OKAY. IF BARRY IS STILL ALIVE--

I WANT TO BE HERE WHEN HE'S FOUND, COMMISSIONER.

EVERY COP ON THE FORCE WILL BE HELPING US.

WE'LL FIND HIM, CLARKSON.

THANK YOU, SIR.

I CAME AS SOON AS I HEARD.

YOU HAVE SOME NERVE COMING HERE.

YOU THINK MY PARTNER IS *MIDNIGHT*?!?

CRACK!

GOT ANY MORE TIPS FROM PSYCHOS YOU WANT TO RUN BY US?!?

DETECTIVE!

CLARKSON. PLEASE.

THIS MIGHT BE AN OPPORTUNE TIME FOR ONE OF YOUR DISAPPEARING ACTS.

I'LL FIND YOUR PARTNER.

I'll need a sample of the blood and mud to run through the Batcomputer...

...but the police <u>don't</u> approve.

It's time to go.

It's time to get back to the <u>cave</u>.

Chapter Two

GOOD EVENING, SIR. I'VE PREPPED THE LAB DATA YOU RADIOED AHEAD.

THANK YOU, ALFRED.

THAT LOOKS BETTER.

I ALSO PREPARED A DRY SUIT.

GOOD. I HAVE A FEELING I'M GOING TO NEED IT. CAN YOU ALSO TAKE OUT THE KEVLAR BODYSUIT 65? THE WATERPROOF ONE.

ARE YOU EXPECTING TO DO BATTLE WITH A TYPHOON THIS EVENING, MASTER BRUCE?

IF ONLY.

AND WHAT MAKES YOU SO SURE KILLER CROC IS BEHIND THE DISAPPEARANCE OF THAT POOR POLICE OFFICER?

HE TORE APART THE CAR. I'D KNOW THOSE CLAW MARKS ANYWHERE.

ANY IDEA WHERE HE MIGHT BE?

I RETRIEVED A MUD SAMPLE FROM THE WRECKAGE. THE GROUND AND AROUND THE CAR WAS MOSTLY CONCRETE, GRAVEL AND SAND. THIS MUD HAD A COMPLETELY DIFFERENT COLOR AND TEXTURE, AND MOST LIKELY CAME FROM KILLER CROC.

THE MUD ALSO HAS ODD COLORS. CHEMICALS. POSSIBLY, PATHOGENS, DETERGENTS OR EVEN OIL.

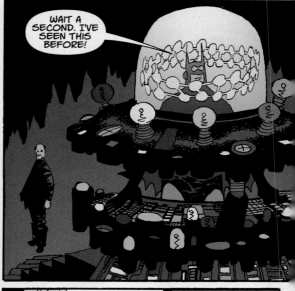

WAIT A SECOND. I'VE SEEN THIS BEFORE!

REMEMBER WHEN BRUCE WAYNE SUED DUNKIRK OVER IMPROPER CHEMICAL WASTE DISPOSAL?

YOU BOYS DO LOVE TO FIGHT.

THAT'S THE SAME TYPE OF TOXIC MUD WE FOUND POURING FROM DUNKIRK'S FACTORIES ON THE WEST SIDE.

AND THERE IT IS.

GOTHAM RIVER

I WAS NOT QUESTIONING YOUR MOTIVATION, MASTER BRUCE. I AM SIMPLY--

"...WORRIED ABOUT YOU."

Chapter Three

Lucas's badge. Damn.

GOTHAM POLICE

The odds of finding him alive are getting less and less likely. And now...

...into the mouth of madness.

The trail leads deeper and deeper underground.

The possibility that Detective Lucas is actually the killer known as Midnight is slim. But Lucas is connected.

And I fear that--

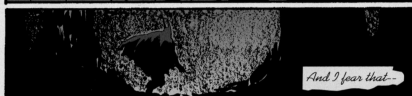

DETECTIVE LUCAS...?

DEAD.

IT'S TOO NEAT, AN OBSESSIVE ATTEMPT AT APPEARING RANDOM.

DID YOU FIND HIM, SIR?

YES. HE'S BEEN SLAUGHTERED.

WOULD YOU LIKE ME TO CONTACT GORDON?

NO. I'M TAKING THE BODY OUT OF HERE. SOMETHING ISN'T RIGHT ABOUT THIS PLACE.

SIR?

IT LOOKS LIKE A VILLAIN LAIR OUT OF A BAD MOVIE. NONE OF THE EQUIPMENT EXCEPT FOR LIGHTS SEEMS TO WORK. IT'S ALL FLASH, FOR SHOW.

WHY WOULD ANYONE GO TO ALL THE TROUBLE?

SOMEBODY LIKE MIDNIGHT...

SOMEBODY WHO WANTS ME TO THINK THEY ARE SOMETHING THEY AREN'T.

I'M SIGNING OFF NOW. I MAY NEED THE CHOPPER, SO STAY CLOSE.

THE JOKER TIPS ME OFF THAT LUCAS IS MIDNIGHT, THEN KILLER CROC KILLS LUCAS AND LEAVES HIM HERE IN THIS FAKE LAIR.

THE JOKER WOULD LIE FOR A MILLION REASONS, BUT WHAT'S CROC'S INTEREST IN ALL OF THIS?

ME?

I'M IN IT FOR THE MEAT.

SNAP!

SNAP!

KRAK!

Chapter Four

HOW DID SOMETHING LIKE THIS HAPPEN? WHY WOULD HE MENTION *MY* NAME TO A REPORTER FROM THE GOTHAM TIMES?! ON WHAT PLANET DOES *THAT* MAKE SENSE?

NOW YOU LISTEN TO *ME!* I WANT YOU TO SHUT THE MOUTHS OF THOSE IDIOTS *AND* THE REPORTERS SO IT'S BUSINESS AS USUAL AND NO ONE'S THE WISER!

WHAT? I'M THE *MAYOR* OF GOTHAM CITY. I CAN DO WHATEVER I WANT!

IDIOT!

GOOD EVENING, MAYOR!

GAH!

IT IS TIME FOR YOUR REIGN OF BRAZEN GLUTTONY AND CORRUPTION TO COME TO AN END.

LOOK, I-- I'M SURE THERE'S SOMETHING I CAN DO FOR YOU...

Chapter Five

RWARRRGH!

SHUNK!

Move past the pain.

Got to incapacitate Croc...

...then I'll figure out his connection to Midnight.

FWAK!

But first, this is going to hurt.

SLLTCH!

ARGH!

YOU READY TO GIVE UP, CROC?

I HAVEN'T EVEN STARTED.

I'M GOING TO CHEW THE FLESH FROM YOUR BONES!

UNGH!

NNNH--

NNRRR--

Chapter Six

NEXT: SILENT
NIGHT,
DEADLY
KNIGHT!

...BUT DETECTIVE BARRY LUCAS WAS ALSO A HUSBAND, A FATHER, AND A PARTNER.

AS WE RELEASE OUR FALLEN BROTHER INTO THE ARMS OF GOD...

FIRE!

BLAM! BLAM! BLAM!

...WE MUST ALSO FACE THE SAD REALITY THAT GOTHAM'S FINEST ARE NOW WITHOUT ONE OF ITS VERY FINEST.

FIRE.

BLAM! BLAM! BLAM! BLAM!

AMEN.

AMEN.

174

BAD DAY FOR COPS, AND I STILL HAVE THE MAYOR'S SERVICE TO ATTEND.

IT'S A BAD DAY FOR GOTHAM. MIDNIGHT IS KILLING WHOLESALE NOW.

AND I'M NO CLOSER TO STOPPING HIM THAN I WAS WHEN HE FIRST APPEARED.

WE HAVE A MOTIVE AND A SUSPECT.

ARE YOU GIVING ME RELATIONSHIP ADVICE, JIM?

I'M OFFERING A FRIEND SOME INFORMATION THAT MIGHT HELP HIM, WHILE LOOKING OUT FOR MY OWN.

WHEN WAS *YOUR* LAST DATE, JIM?

I'M A BUSY MAN.

SO AM I.

THAT DIDN'T STOP YOU FROM EMBRACING A DETECTIVE IN THE MIDDLE OF A CRIME SCENE.

YES, THAT WAS... STRANGE. AND UNEXPECTED.

STRANGE, INDEED. I'LL HAVE A WORD WITH CLARKSON WHEN THINGS SETTLE DOWN A BIT. YOU KNOW I ONCE MET HER--

--FATHER.

Chapter Two

HAHAHAHAHAHA!

NURSE! NURSE! WHERE'S MY JELL-O?

DOES HE *EVER* STOP?

NO, NOT REALLY.

HEY, NURSE! YOU HEAR ME? COME ON! I WON'T TRY TO BITE YOU...*AGAIN*...I PROOOOOMISE!

HAHAHAHAHAHA!

KEEP IT UP AND I'LL MUZZLE YOU!

SLAM!

JOKER.

OH, YOU CAME TO VISIT!

POP!

WHUMPF!

179

JUST SHUT UP AND LET ME TALK. BLINK FOR YES, STARE AT ME LIKE A PSYCHOPATH FOR NO.

YOU GOT DUPED BY MIDNIGHT, RIGHT?

YOU THINK YOU WERE DRUGGED?

HRN.

OKAY, I'M GOING TO NEED...

...A *BLOOD* SAMPLE.

THE BELLY WOUND WILL HEAL, BUT IT HURTS, DOESN'T IT? YOU SHOULD KNOW, YOU'VE INFLICTED *ENOUGH* OF THEM.

AND WHEN YOU GET BACK TO ARKHAM, YOU HAVE A NEW SECURED CELL WAITING. TRY TO BEHAVE.

Chapter Three

THREE DAYS UNTIL CHRISTMAS.

BRIIING!

WAYNE RESIDENCE. ALFRED PENNYWORTH SPEAKING. OH, HELLO, MISS CLARKSON. NO, I'M AFRAID MISTER WAYNE IS AWAY AT THE MOMENT.

DEC 22

WE WERE SUPPOSED TO HAVE DINNER TONIGHT...

...AND I'M AFRAID I WON'T BE ABLE TO MAKE IT.

THOMAS WAYNE

WOULD YOU PLEASE GIVE BRUCE THE MESSAGE?

OF COURSE I WILL. MISTER WAYNE WILL BE MOST DISAPPOINTED.

MERRY CHRISTMAS.

HOW DID HE TAKE IT?

LUCKILY I ONLY HAD TO TALK TO THE BUTLER.

HOW ARE YOU FEELING?

BETTER.

NOW.

CHRISTMAS EVE.

COME IN.

TAP TAP TAP

COMMISSIONER JAMES GORDON

Chapter Four

HERE'S BARRY'S AUTOPSY REPORT.

ANYTHING USEFUL?

NOTHING WE DIDN'T ALREADY KNOW.

IF IT'S OKAY WITH YOU, SIR, I'D LIKE TO TAKE ANOTHER PERSONAL DAY.

I SAID YOU CAME BACK TOO SOON. IT'S CHRISTMAS, CLARKSON. TAKE THE REST OF THE WEEK.

THE DAY WILL BE FINE, SIR.

WHAT'S IT SAY?

I REALLY WISH YOU WOULDN'T DO THAT...

IT SAYS THAT HE DIED OF TRAUMA DUE TO BLOOD LOSS...WOUNDS MOST LIKELY MADE BY ANIMAL-LIKE CLAWS. IT WAS CROC.

THEN THE REPORT IS *WRONG*, JIM. THERE'S MORE TO THIS. EITHER YOUR M.E. ISN'T AS SHARP AS HE USED TO BE...

...OR SOMEBODY DOCTORED THE REPORT. THERE WERE SOME TRACES OF ORGANIC MATERIAL, BUT I ALSO FOUND METAL FRAGMENTS.

MIDNIGHT KILLED LUCAS.

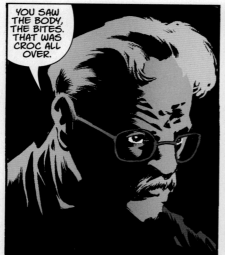

YOU SAW THE BODY, THE BITES. THAT WAS CROC ALL OVER.

THE BITES WERE POST-MORTEM, JIM.

THEN WHAT'S YOUR THEORY?

I THINK WE HAVE TO CONSIDER THE OPTION THAT IT MIGHT BE AN INSIDE JOB.

MIDNIGHT'S A COP, JIM. IT'S THE *ONLY* EXPLANATION.

BRIIING!

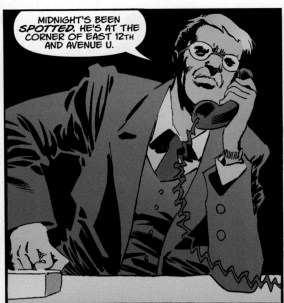

MIDNIGHT'S BEEN *SPOTTED.* HE'S AT THE CORNER OF EAST 12TH AND AVENUE U.

I'M ON MY WAY.

POLICE

Chapter Five

THANK YOU! MERRY CHRISTMAS! HAPPY NEW YEAR!

AND MERRY CHRISTMAS TO *ME!*

GIVE

GURK!

SPLTCH!

RUN! RUN! YOU'RE ALL **CORRUPT!** YOU'RE ALL GOING TO--

BAMM!

ENOUGH!

KRAK!

THOK!

YOU'D **BETTER** WATCH OUT, BATMAN!

I SEE YOU WHEN YOU'RE SLEEPING...

DISTEFANO MORTUARY

HE CALLS HIS CHILDREN BY NAME

He's going after _all_ of the cops who were working the investigation.

WHPP-CRACK!!

CATWOMAN?!?

FWOOSH!!

UNGH!

NO--

APRIL!!

SHRRRIPP!

RRRAAGH!

HOLD ON, APRIL, I'M--

Chapter
One

SHE'S GONE, OLD FRIEND. LET THEM DO THEIR JOB.

SHE'S DEAD BECAUSE OF ME.

SHE'S DEAD BECAUSE SHI WAS A POLICE OFFICER. MAYBE SHE WAS CLOSE TO DISCOVERING WHO MIDNIGHT REALLY IS.

TO MAKE MATTERS WORSE, MIDNIGHT'S REIGN OF TERROR SEEMS TO BE HAVING AN EFFECT. CRIME, ACROSS THE BOARD, IS DOWN ALL OVER GOTHAM.

CRIME HAS DROPPED BECAUSE PEOPLE ARE AFRAID, JIM. CRIMINALS *AND* THEIR VICTIMS.

AGREED.

WATCH YOUR BACK, JIM. MIDNIGHT'S GOING WAY OUTSIDE HIS M.O. NOW. YOU COULD BECOME A TARGET.

JUST FIND HIM AND STOP HIM.

I CAN HANDLE MYSELF.

Chapter Two

SIR, I JUST HEARD THE--

I NEED TO STAY FOCUSED, ALFRED. MIDNIGHT IS TRYING TO WEAKEN ME BY ATTACKING THE PEOPLE AROUND ME.

DID YOU COMPARE THE JOKER'S BLOOD SAMPLE WITH MAN-BAT'S AND CRANE'S?

I DID, BUT I'M NOT SURE WHAT I'M SUPPOSED TO BE LOOKING FOR, SIR.

ANYTHING ABNORMAL.

HMMM.

I'VE INCREASED THE MAGNIFICATION. TELL ME WHAT YOU SEE.

DO YOU SEE THEM?

SMALL WHITE CYLINDERS. THEY APPEAR TO BE MUCH SMALLER THAN THE CELLS THEMSELVES.

WHAT ARE THEY?

I'VE NEVER SEEN ANYTHING LIKE IT, BUT THEY APPEAR TO BE SYNTHETIC, SOMETHING THAT WAS INTRODUCED INTO THE BLOODSTREAM.

TO SERVE WHAT PURPOSE?

IT'S CLEAR THAT SCARECROW AND MAN-BAT WERE NOT QUITE THEMSELVES. THEY APPEARED DRUGGED, BUT IT'S HARD TO CONTROL A DRUGGED SUBJECT.

IT APPEARS AS IF THE JOKER WAS ALSO DRUGGED, BUT WITH UNSATISFACTORY RESULTS.

I THINK WHAT WE ARE LOOKING AT IS A SYNTHETIC CONTROL MECHANISM, AND I SUSPECT THEY ARE CURRENTLY INACTIVE.

THEN WHAT *ACTIVATES* THE MECHANISM?

THAT IS THE QUESTION, ISN'T IT?

CHRISTMAS CARDS, SIR?

I FOUND THEM IN APRIL CLARKSON'S MAILBOX. I THOUGHT I'D BETTER REMOVE BRUCE WAYNE FROM THE INVESTIGATION AS MUCH AS POSSIBLE. THE OTHERS ARE FROM A RELATIVE AND DUNKIRK.

I NEED YOU TO WORK ON A FEW THINGS WHILE I'M GONE. FIRST, START EXPOSING THE BLOOD SAMPLES TO AN ARRAY OF RAYS; X-RAY, INFRARED, MICROWAVE, RADIO, T-RAYS, MAGNETIC AND GAMMA. SEE IF ANY CAUSE A REACTION.

VERY GOOD, SIR. AND THE OTHER?

RUN A FULL BACKGROUND CHECK ON DUNKIRK. HIS NAME HAS COME UP ONE TOO MANY TIMES.

BUT, ALFRED... MERRY CHRISTMAS.

OF COURSE.

AND WHERE WILL I FIND YOU?

PEOPLE ARE DYING. I DON'T HAVE THE LUXURY OF TAKING THE NIGHT OFF.

I HAVE SOMETHING BRUCE WAYNE MIGHT BE BETTER SUITED TO LOOK INTO.

SIR... MASTER BRUCE... I KNOW HOW DIFFICULT LOSING MS. CLARKSON MUST BE, BUT I IMPLORE YOU TO LET THINGS REST FOR TONIGHT. TONIGHT OF *ALL* NIGHTS.

Chapter Three

WAREHOUSE

PIER 12

OKAY, SO WE'RE ALL HERE.

BUT WHERE IS THIS MIDNIGHT FREAK?

WHAT AN HONOR IT IS TO MEET ALL OF GOTHAM'S TOP CRIME BOSSES.

I TRUST YOU DID AS I ASKED AND ARRIVED ALONE AND UNARMED.

HERE I AM, GENTLEMEN.

Chapter Four

EAST GOTHAM COUNTY.

DING DONG!

YES?

WALTER CLARKSON?

THAT'S ME. CAN I HELP YOU?

I ASSUME YOU'VE BEEN NOTIFIED ABOUT YOUR NIECE, APRIL CLARKSON.

APRIL? NOTIFIED?

OH NO.

I'M SO SORRY. I THOUGHT THE POLICE DEPARTMENT WOULD HAVE TOLD YOU BY NOW.

YOU'RE NOT A COP?

NO, I'M A FRIEND. I'M SORRY YOU HAD TO FIND OUT THIS WAY.

GOTHAM GAZETTE
MIDNITE RAMPAGE!

I'M NOT SURPRISED. I WASN'T ON HER NEXT OF KIN. I HAVEN'T SEEN OR HEARD FROM APRIL SINCE SHE ENTERED THE POLICE ACADEMY.

BUT YOU SENT HER CARDS?

HABIT, I GUESS. IT'S HARD TO LET GO OF FAMILY...EVEN WHEN THEY SEEM TO BE ABLE TO LET GO OF YOU.

I GUESS I DIDN'T KNOW HER THAT WELL. SHE LIVED HERE?

NOT LONG. HER FATHER, MY BROTHER, WAS KILLED WHEN SHE WAS 17. SHE WAS OUT OF HERE THE DAY OF HER 18TH BIRTHDAY.

YOUR BROTHER WAS A GREAT MAN.

THAT'S WHAT THEY SAY NOW.

WHY ARE YOU HERE, MISTER?

I...I SUPPOSE BECAUSE I MISS HER.

I WISH I COULD HELP YOU, BUT APRIL DIDN'T STAY IN CONTACT. SHE WAS LIKE THAT. I'M SORRY.

930

MAYBE YOU SHOULD TAKE THIS, MR. WAYNE.

YOU *KNOW* ME?

WHO IN GOTHAM DOESN'T?

IT'S THE LAST OF THE THINGS SHE LEFT BEHIND. I'D RATHER YOU HAVE IT THAN THE OTHER FELLOW.

OTHER?

SORRY, I LIED ABOUT NOT KNOWING, BUT I THOUGHT YOU WERE ONE OF *DUNKIRK'S* FRIENDS. HE CAME BY TOO, ASKING QUESTIONS AND OFFERING MONEY FOR A FANCY HEADSTONE.

I SEE.

It makes sense.

Midnight is copying Batman. Why wouldn't Dunkirk copy Wayne?

Does that mean Midnight knows that Wayne and Batman are one?

If he knew, Midnight would have hit hard and personal. He's hurting those close to Batman--not Wayne--so it's safe to assume he _doesn't_ know.

Too many people are dead because of Midnight's murderous rampage.

As much as I want to hurt him for what he did to April...I have to resist.

IT'S OVER.

YOU HAD ME FOOLED FOR A WHILE, BUT I'M ON TO YOU NOW, DUN--

I'm forced to admit it: I've failed.

Midnight has been one step ahead of me all along. He's toying with me now.

If I'm Gotham's only hope...then I fear that all hope is lost.

Midnight is loose somewhere in my city. Free to prey upon both the innocent and the guilty. Free to terrify and terrorize.
"FROM A PROUD TOWER IN THE TOWN, DEATH LOOKS GIGANTICALLY DOWN."
HA! I HAVE DONE IT!

AND THERE SHE IS.

I come back to her old diary--a keepsake presented to Bruce Wayne by her estranged uncle. It is now my only connection to April Clarkson.

FROM DADDY FOR MY SIXTEENTH B-DAY!

DETECTIVE JOHN CLARKSON MURDERED

HEROIC COP'S DEATH "A LIFE LOST..."

Her father's obituary. John Clarkson. A hero cop killed in an incident off-duty. He was a popular public servant whose murder shocked the city and orphaned his only child. The irony is not lost on me.

I'M SORRY ABOUT YOUR PARTNER. I DID EVERYTHING I COULD, APRIL.

I BECAME A COP TO *HELP* PEOPLE, NOT TO WATCH MORE OF THEM *DIE.*

I *HATE* THIS CITY...

I put on the cape and cowl for the same reason--to make sure that no one else suffered the same fate as my parents...or myself.

I won't fail them...or April.

Chapter Two

IN MEMORY OF APRIL CLARKSON FALLEN NOT FORGOTTEN BADGE 714

REST IN PEACE, APRIL...

...I'LL MAKE SURE MIDNIGHT PAYS FOR HIS CRIMES. YOUR DEATH *WILL* BE AVENGED.

WAYNE?

OH. GOOD AFTERNOON, COMMISSIONER.

I DIDN'T MEAN TO INTERRUPT. I JUST WANTED TO PAY MY RESPECTS. I CAN COME BACK LATER IF--

--NO, IT'S ALL RIGHT, COMMISSIONER.

I WAS JUST LEAVING.

WAIT A MINUTE, SON. YOU REALLY CARED FOR HER, DIDN'T YOU?

SHE WAS...

YES. YES I DID. MORE THAN I EVEN THOUGHT.

SHE WAS A GOOD COP, JUST LIKE HER OLD MAN. DAMN SHAME, TRAGEDY WIPING OUT HER ENTIRE FAMILY LIKE THAT.

NOT HER ENTIRE FAMILY, COMMISSIONER. HER UNCLE IS STILL ALIVE.

REALLY? I WASN'T AWARE THAT SHE HAD ANY OTHER FAMILY LEFT.

I GUESS YOU TWO WERE CLOSER THAN I THOUGHT.

I'M SO SORRY FOR YOUR LOSS, MR. WAYNE.

AND I YOURS, COMMISSIONER.

BRUCE WAYNE... I THINK YOUR **HEART** BREAKS. PERHAPS I CAN HELP YOU WITH THAT...

Chapter Three

It's midnight in Gotham City, and her streets are empty.

No people.

No crime.

No nothing.

Where is Midnight?

IT'S GLORIOUS. ABSOLUTELY GLORIOUS.

I HAVE HIM RIGHT WHERE I WANT HIM.

EXCUSE ME, SIR, BUT I'VE RUN THE TESTS ON THOSE BLOOD SAMPLES THAT YOU ASKED ME TO ANALYZE. THE RESULTS ARE ALL NEGATIVE.

I'M ON MY WAY, ALFRED.

THIS IS IT, MY DEAR. OUR TIME HAS COME.

PURRRFECT, MIDNIGHT. I'LL GATHER THE OTHERS...

Chapter Four

There must be an answer.

A small, synthetic control mechanism was introduced into the bloodstreams of Scarecrow, Axe-Man, Croc, Catwoman and even the Joker. But I still don't know what *activates* these mechanisms...

...and more important, what *stops* them.

But I *will*.

I WAS LOOKING FOR *ONE* THING, BUT I WAS WRONG. IT'S EVERYTHING, ALFRED. *ALL* OF THE RAYS, COMBINED IN DIFFERENT INCREMENTS, VARIED TO EACH SPECIFIC BLOOD TYPE.

AND WHAT OF THE JOKER?

HIS BLOOD'S ALREADY CONTAMINATED. HE WAS DRUGGED BY MIDNIGHT, BUT THE MECHANISM NEVER TOOK EFFECT. HE'S TOO FAR GONE.

LOOK--THIS IS IT--I WAS RIGHT! I'VE ISOLATED THE TRIGGERING MECHANISM, AND CAN REVERSE IT. I CAN BLOCK THE SIGNAL.

COME ON, ALFRED. WE'VE GOT A LOT OF WORK TO DO, AND VERY LITTLE TIME IN WHICH TO DO IT.

NOW HE NEEDS MY HELP...

SOON, MY DEAR, VERY SOON, EVEN THE BATMAN WILL **FEAR** ME!

I THOUGHT WE WERE GOING TO *KILL* HIM? THE ARRANGEMENTS HAVE BEEN MADE...?

ALL IN GOOD TIME, MY DEAR.

I WILL GIVE **HIM** THE OPTION, BUT I KNOW, IN MY HEART, HIS ANSWER. AND SO, HE WILL FEAR ME, AS SO MANY HAVE FEARED HIM. THEN HE WILL KNEEL...AND HE WILL **KNOW**. AND FINALLY, WHEN I HAVE DECIDED THAT THE TIME IS RIGHT, THE BATMAN WILL **DIE**.

BUT FIRST, THERE IS ONE MORE HEART FOR US TO TAKE: BRUCE WAYNE'S!

YOU CAN KEEP HIS TICKER. I'LL TAKE HIS CASH AND JEWELS.

WHATEVER YOUR PRETTY LITTLE HEART DESIRES.

CLARKSON

AND WHAT DO YOU THINK WAYNE'S HEART DESIRES?

Chapter Six

WHERE IS HE!?!

DESTROYING EXPENSIVE EQUIPMENT WILL NOT HELP IN YOUR SEARCH FOR THE MENACING MIDNIGHT, SIR.

WHAMM!

NOR WILL THESE ADOLESCENT TEMPER TANTRUMS OR YOUR RECENT PROCLIVITY TO SULKING ABOUT THIS DRAFTY OLD CAVE, BOTH OF WHICH I'M SURE YOUR PARENTS WOULD NOT APPROVE.

WAYNE

FURTHERMORE, I DO NOT APPRECIATE HAVING TO CLEAN UP AFTER YOU.

I KNOW YOU'RE HURTING, SIR, BOTH PROFESSIONALLY, FOR LACK OF A BETTER WORD, AND PERSONALLY. BUT DON'T LET YOUR *HEART* GO BLACK, SIR. DON'T CROSS THAT LINE, BRUCE.

ALFRED, I... THANK YOU.

I CAME AS SOON AS I GOT YOUR SIGNAL.

I THOUGHT IT'D BE SAFER FOR US TO MEET UP HERE, WHERE WE CAN TALK FREELY, AWAY FROM EVERYONE AND EVERYTHING.

I THOUGHT I MIGHT'VE BEEN MIDNIGHT'S NEXT TARGET--AND I MIGHT STILL BE ON HIS HIT LIST--BUT I THINK WE KNOW *WHO* HIS NEXT VICTIM WILL BE.

A VALENTINE'S HEART?

AND AN EXPENSIVE ONE AT THAT. THE CANDIES ARE CALLED "MIDNIGHT MYSTERY." THEY'RE A HIGH-END VARIETY OF DARK CHOCOLATES MADE BY MADELEINE SOPHIE, BRUCE WAYNE'S PERSONAL CHOCOLATIER.

OH, NO...

DID YOUR MEN RUN A DNA TEST?

YES. THEY MADE A QUICK TEST OF THE DRIED BLOOD. IT... IT MATCHES CLARKSON'S DNA.

"THEY WERE DISCOVERED ON HER GRAVESTONE. I HAD BEEN THERE EARLIER, AND SO HAD WAYNE. I'M SORRY, MY FRIEND."

HE'S TAUNTING ME.

NO, HE'S TARGETING WAYNE.

I'VE INSTRUCTED THE PILOT TO TAKE US TO WAYNE TOWER. MY GUT'S TELLING ME THAT THAT'S WHERE HE'S GOING TO STRIKE.

AND WAYNE?

HOME IN HIS MANOR WITH "BAMBI," ACCORDING TO HIS BUTLER. I'VE GOT SQUAD CARS SURROUNDING HIS HOUSE, JUST IN CASE.

BUT STATELY WAYNE MANOR IS TOO FAR FROM THE CITY. MIDNIGHT WILL BE *HERE*.

AGREED. AND HE'S ALL MINE, JIM.

Smart thinking on Alfred's part to give Bruce Wayne an alibi. But Gordon's right: Midnight is targeting Wayne, but he's also sending me a message.

One way or another, this ends tonight.

...I WANT YOU TO JOIN ME.

YOU'RE MAD.

AS ARE YOU...YET YOU REFUSE TO FACE REALITY.

YOU'VE SEEN WHAT'S BECOME OF GOTHAM. WHAT I HAVE DONE. I HAVE USED THE NIGHT--I HAVE USED FEAR--TO BRING ORDER TO GOTHAM CITY! BUT IT'S NOT ENOUGH TO SIMPLY STOP CRIME.

THOSE WHO STAND IN OUR WAY MUST BE ELIMINATED. ONLY THEN WILL GOTHAM REACH ITS ZENITH!

BRUCE WAYNE WILL BE YOUR FIRST VICTIM.

DESTROY HIM. KILL THE BOY WHO BETRAYED HIS FATHER'S TRUST, THE PLAYBOY WHO WASTES HIS DAYS, AND GOTHAM WILL KNOW THAT NEITHER THE ELITE NOR THE SCUM WILL HAVE SANCTUARY HERE.

BRUCE WAYNE'S DEATH AT YOUR HANDS WILL SIGNIFY THE DAWN OF A NEW AGE IN GOTHAM!

WAYNE

YOU LACK THE ONE THING THAT GIVES TRUE STRENGTH.

YOU'RE BLINDED BY MADNESS. YOUR "LAW" REQUIRES PEOPLE TO LIVE IN FEAR. YOUR "ORDER" BRINGS ONLY TERROR AND PANIC.

YOU'RE *NOTHING* LIKE ME. YOU LIVE BY REVENGE, NOT JUSTICE.

YOU HAVE NO *PITY.*

AND YOU HAVE NO *HEART!*

NOT SO FAST!

WREEEEEEEEEEE

Alfred and I were able to isolate and reverse the triggering mechanism that Midnight injected into their bloodstreams. In other words, this is now a fair fight.

A few well-placed smoke bombs will disorient them long enough for me to make my move.

MIDNIGHT!

YOU CANNOT RUN FROM ME!

The innocent citizens of Gotham are scared. Midnight has held them in his icy grip, but that ends now--tonight.

The people of Gotham need to be reminded that there is always hope. And to do that, they need a symbol.

But the criminals of Gotham must remain superstitious and cowardly. They must see the symbol--and they must fear me.

And they will fear me.

246

YES, THERE HAVE BEEN DEVELOPMENTS SINCE HE CAME TO ME.

The fear serum has changed. Midnight must've altered it in some way. It doesn't seem to be inducing fear, but it is causing hallucinations. I need to get it out of my lungs--fast.

WHAT'S THE MATTER, BATMAN? IS YOUR WORLD TURNING UPSIDE DOWN?

ENOUGH GAMES!

SHOW YOURSELF, MIDNIGHT-- *FACE ME!*

ALL IN GOOD TIME, MY DEAR, ALL IN GOOD TIME.

Chapter Two

GRRRR...

I GIVE, I GIVE. DON'T SHOOT...

HANDS UP, CREEP, OR WE'RE ALL GONNA BE WEARING NEW SHOES.

BATMAN-- BEHIND YOU!

KRAK!

OOMPF!

THANKS, JIM.

YOU OKAY?

I WILL BE ONCE I CLEAR THE TOXIN OUT OF MY LUNGS. AND JIM--

--KEEP A CELL OPEN FOR MIDNIGHT. I'M BRINGING HIM IN.

GOOD LUCK, OLD FRIEND.

He's headed towards the old section of town. To historic Gotham.

THAT'S IT! FOLLOW YOUR **HEART**, BATMAN, WHILE YOU STILL HAVE ONE!

He's leading me here, but _why?_ What does he have planned?

GOTHAM HISTORICAL SITE

VAN TASSEL FAMILY FARM & WINDMILL

FOUNDED BY DUTCH IMMIGRANT JOHN VAN TASSEL IN 1761, THE 90-ACRE VAN TASSEL FAMILY FARM AND WINDMILL WAS ONCE THE HEART OF GOTHAM'S

"LO! DEATH HAS REARED HIMSELF A THRONE, IN A STRANGE CITY LYING ALONE!"

IT'S OVER, MIDNIGHT. THERE'S NO ESCAPE.

YOU PRESUME THAT I WANT TO ESCAPE, BUT YOU ARE **WRONG.**

I BROUGHT YOU HERE--TO WHERE GOTHAM CITY **BEGAN**--FOR A REASON. DID YOU NOT REALIZE THAT I--

--ENOUGH. TALKING.

Chapter Three

257

NEVER.

Midnight's right. I'm still disoriented from Crane's intensified fear gas, so it's time for me to blow a little smoke of my own.

YOU ATTEMPT TO RUN FROM ME, COWARD?

WHIFFF!

I'M NOT RUNNING ANYWHERE, MIDNIGHT.

YOU **CAN'T**, CAPED CRUSADER. YOUR HEAD IS STILL SPINNING, ISN'T IT?

TELL ME, BATMAN, HAVE YOU STARTED SEEING THINGS YET?

APRIL...

BUT... YOU'RE DEAD...?

NOT QUITE, SWEETIE...

...BUT I AM TO DIE FOR!

AND I DON'T APPRECIATE BEING TAKEN ADVANTAGE OF!

WHIPP-CRACKK!

KER-

FWASSHH!

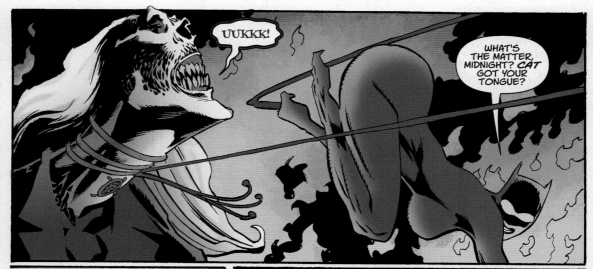

NEXT:
THE GRAND
(GUIGNOL)
FINALE

It's all happening in slow motion.

Midnight lured me to Old Gotham, in order for me to watch him burn down the very foundations upon which Gotham City was built.

I can't allow that to happen.

But my head is still spinning from Scarecrow's fear gas. It's making me see things. It's making me see her.

It's making me see April.

TIME'S UP, BATMAN!

BLAK!

NO!

DAFF!

BATMAM CREATED BY BOB KANE

As the old Windmill goes up in flames, I can already hear the sirens of Gotham's Fire Department. They'll be here within minutes to contain the blaze.

It's Midnight's whereabouts that concern me.

His cloak flutters on the breeze, like a bat returning to its cave at dawn.

Like me.

And I know, at least for now, that the monster that has plagued these streets--my streets--is gone.

But the case is far from over; the mystery not yet solved.

I will know the truth.

Chapter Two

LOOK! THE WINDMILL! THIS IS *MIDNIGHT'S* DOING!

SURELY HE *DIED* IN THE BLAST, OR IS *ROASTING ALIVE* IN THE FIRE!

NO ONE COULD SURVIVE THAT! LOOK AT IT GO!

NO, *YOU LOOK*-- SOMEONE *DID* SURVIVE. THERE--!!!

--IT'S *BATMAN!!!*

It's midnight in Gotham City, and for the first time in a long while, there seems to be hope.

The cane and top hat are all that remain of Midnight's reign of terror. They will be useful in uncovering the mystery that continues to haunt me.

BATMAN...

BATMAN...

SON, ARE YOU ALL RIGHT?

I SAW HER, JIM. I SAW *APRIL*. I SAW HER BURNING ALIVE IN THE FIRE.

YOU'RE STILL UNDER CRANE'S INFLUENCE. DETECTIVE CLARKSON IS DEAD.

YOUR WORK HERE IS DONE, MY FRIEND. YOU'VE DONE MORE THAN ANY ONE MAN COULD, OR SHOULD. GO HOME.

BESIDES... IT'S ALMOST DAWN.

GO GET SOME...

...SLEEP?

Chapter Three

THE NEXT NIGHT.

The _signal_. I'm needed at police headquarters.

Perhaps Gordon's men found the body.

Perhaps this case is at long last solved, and the innocent dead can finally rest in peace.

Perhaps...

MY MEN SEARCHED THE ENTIRE AREA. THEN I HAD THEM SEARCH IT AGAIN, AND AGAIN AFTER THAT. THE ONLY THING THAT SURVIVED THAT BLAST IS _YOU_.

THE DEPUTY MAYOR AND DISTRICT ATTORNEY ARE OFFICIALLY DECLARING THIS CASE _CLOSED_.

...or perhaps not.

I DON'T LIKE IT ANY BETTER THAN YOU, BUT THE CITIZENS OF GOTHAM SAW MIDNIGHT CONSUMED IN THE BLAST. THEY SAW THE VAN TASSEL WINDMILL EXPLODE AND _YOU_ FLY AWAY. THEY BELIEVE GOTHAM TO BE _SAFE_ AGAIN.

I WISH THEY WERE RIGHT...

...BUT THIS _ISN'T_ OVER, JIM.

Chapter Four

It's a Catch-22. Every lead is a dead end; every dead end a new mystery.

I've been over every angle... every possible motivation, reason, and rationale, but to no avail.

I've got to retrace every step of the investigation. I've got to go back to the beginning.

It started with Scarecrow attempting to steal the Hand of Glory, and Man-Bat actually stealing the Skull of Ra. But it was never about the supernatural. Those were just red herrings to throw the police off the trail, and to distract me. It worked.

I have to remove all of the true red herrings--all of the actual dead ends--if I'm to solve this case. And all of the villains I fought were just that: red herrings.

Scarecrow. Axe-Man. Man-Bat. Clayface. Joker. Killer Croc. Catwoman. All of them were drugged and manipulated by Midnight. All of them were used by Midnight to mask his true intentions; to keep me busy while Midnight was loose on the streets, killing. None of the villains have any real connection to Midnight.

If the criminals aren't yielding any results, then the answer to "Who is Midnight?" must lie with the victims.

ANY LUCK ON THE CASE, SIR?

NOT YET, ALFRED, THOUGH ONE POSSIBLE LEAD SUGGESTS THAT APRIL'S FATHER IS SOMEHOW INVOLVED...

I spend the next several hours poring through the boxes given to me by April's Uncle, John Clarkson's brother. I read through April's high school yearbook and diary, as well as old cards and letters, and suddenly, everything changes.

It was personal. It was *always* personal. Midnight was connected to *all* of the victims.

APRIL'S DIARY

CASA ROBLE YEARBOOK

And so was Clarkson's family.

Could Midnight have killed April for something her father--or her uncle--did in the past?

What were the sins of the father, and why were they passed on to his daughter?

The GCPD mainframe leads me to a deleted file on John Clarkson. Seems as if the Mayor was a close friend of John Clarkson's, back when John had just made Detective and the Mayor was the D.A. The Mayor's name also came up in a Christmas card to the Clarkson family back when April was 10.

The deleted file also sheds some light onto how John Clarkson rose through the ranks so quickly. He did it the same way everyone else did in Gotham back then: by planting evidence, falsifying convictions, and heavy kickbacks. And it was all covered up.

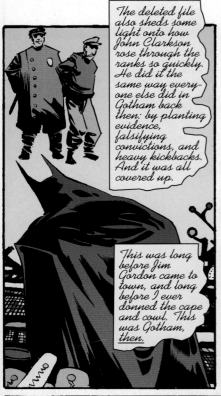

This was long before Jim Gordon came to town, and long before I ever donned the cape and cowl. This was Gotham, then.

John Clarkson never hesitated to bend the law to put a criminal behind bars. His career was filled with medals and awards because, despite _his_ twisted sense of vigilante justice, he was perceived a hero to all who knew him.

And when a bullet ended his career, his adoring public demanded justice for their fallen martyr. But when no suspect was found, the papers said that only Clarkson himself could've found his killer. All of this led the police to name their highest award in _his_ honor.

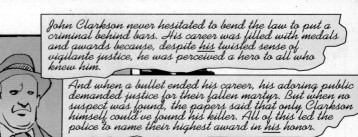

DET JOHN CLARKSON MEMORIAL AWARD

John Clarkson was everything that was wrong with Gotham, and his secret went with him to his grave, as did his files, which were buried deeper than six feet under. Not even Gordon knew how far this went. So who did?

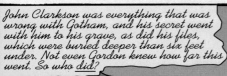

John Clarkson's brother didn't believe the hype. He told me so when I went to pay my respects. But what about April? Is that why _she_ joined the force? Was she following in her father's footsteps?

Or was Clarkson's death--No.

No. No. No.

I tell myself that it's not possible, but _anything's_ possible. I need _proof_ in order to discredit my _theory_.

The car goes from 0 to 80 in 2.2 seconds. It's _not_ fast enough.

275

Midnight's hired thugs were snitches for John Clarkson. Sgt. Henderson was a drunk and an embarrassment to the badge.

The victims on the billboard were all associates of Clarkson--family friends, neighbors, coworkers--and they were deemed corrupt.

LORRAINE'S BBQ

OPEN

Dunkirk was a shady businessman who tried to court April. He was also another red herring to throw me off the case.

And the Detective who figured it all out first was the late Barry Lucas, April's partner.

But April's uncle remained unharmed. Why? There are only two possibilities.

Chapter Five

My answers lie here--with the dead.

This is supposed to be a solemn, holy place; a place for final rest.

Instead, it is to me a symbol of regret and failure.

And I fear that my greatest regret--my greatest failure--lies beneath the dirt.

And if so, what does that say of me?

I don't want to open the box. In this instance, I no longer want to learn the truth.

I open the casket and see the remains of April's charred body.

I know her uncle is too old and too out of shape to be running around Gotham, going toe-to-toe with me.

More important, I know his record is clean...I know that he is innocent.

That means that he cannot be Midnight.

And that means only one thing.

And the DNA confirms it.

NO MATCH

Blood and bone do not lie.

Heaven forgive me, but I wish that she really was dead.

But she's not.

NO.

The uplink to the Bat-computer confirms the truth--the woman in that grave is not April Clarkson.

April Clarkson is Midnight.

The body belongs to Karen Beckett, a "lady of the night" who went missing several months ago. Her physical description matches April's perfectly.

I can only presume that April used some of her own blood on the heart that was left atop Wayne Tower. It's also safe to assume that she falsified her own coroner's report.

And despite what Gordon's men think, I know that the fire didn't kill her. And that means that April Clarkson-- that Midnight--is still alive.

NO.

ALFRED... IT WAS *HER*. IT WAS HER ALL ALONG. APRIL WAS MIDNIGHT.

SHE STAGED HER OWN DEATH BEFORE MY VERY EYES.

YES, SIR. I GOT YOUR MESSAGE. I AM SO SORRY, MASTER BRUCE.

IT IS A TRULY TRAGIC ENDING, SIR, AND A VERY PAINFUL LESSON LEARNED.

NOW IS *NOT* THE TIME FOR A LECTURE, ALFRED. I'LL HANDLE THIS ON MY *OWN*.

THE *HELL* YOU WILL. YOU'VE SHUT OUT EVERYONE SINCE THIS AFFAIR FIRST BEGAN, AND IT HAS COST GOTHAM DEARLY. I WILL NOT LET YOU CONTINUE DOWN THIS MISANTHROPIC ROAD OF YOURS.

ALFRED, I--

NO, NOW IS THE TIME FOR YOU TO *LISTEN*, MASTER BRUCE. IF YOU ARE TO CONTINUE THIS NIGHTLY CRUSADE AGAINST CRIME, THEN YOU MUST DO IT *RIGHT*, OR YOU WILL SURELY DO IT *ALONE*.

I DON'T UNDERSTAND...?

PRECISELY. YOU FELL IN *LOVE*, AND THAT IS WONDERFUL. IT IS SOMETHING THAT I HAVE HOPED AND PRAYED FOR. I THOUGHT THAT LOVE MIGHT CAUSE YOU TO HANG UP YOUR CAPE AND COWL, AND NOW I FEAR THAT IT WILL ONLY REDOUBLE YOUR EFFORTS.

YES, BECAUSE I *FAILED* HER.

NO, YOU FAILED *YOURSELF*. LIKE MOST HUMAN BEINGS, YOU WERE BLINDED BY LOVE. BUT UNLIKE MOST PEOPLE, YOU NEVER SHARED YOUR FEELINGS WITH ANYONE. WHEN I INQUIRED ABOUT YOU AND MISS CLARKSON, YOU DENIED IT TO ME LIKE A GUILTY YOUNG SCHOOLBOY.

AND AS SHE IS THE DAUGHTER OF A SLAIN PARENT WHO ENTERED INTO LAW ENFORCEMENT WITH A SINGLE-MINDED OBSESSION, I THOUGHT THAT A MORE THAN CURSORY CHECK INTO MISS CLARKSON'S BACKGROUND MIGHT BE REQUIRED. AS YOU ARE NO DOUBT AWARE, I *DO* HAVE SOME EXPERIENCE WITH THOSE TYPES.

AND AS SHE WAS THE LEAD DETECTIVE ON A MULTIPLE MURDER CASE, MIXING BUSINESS WITH PLEASURE WAS NEVER A WAY TO HELP END THOSE ATROCITIES. EVEN THE COMMISSIONER KNEW THAT.

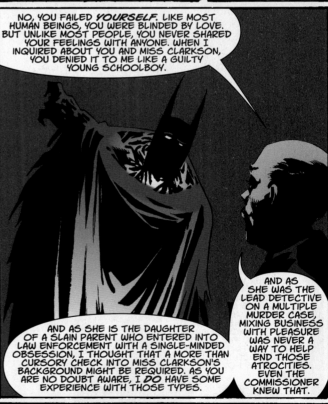

BUT I *NEVER*--

YOU HAVE BEEN ALONE A LONG TIME, MASTER BRUCE, AND I FEAR THAT UNTIL YOU STOP WEARING THIS GET UP, YOU WILL REMAIN SO.

YOUR CRUSADE HAS MADE YOU VULNERABLE IN MATTERS OF THE HEART. YOU WERE NOT ABLE TO PROPERLY DO YOUR JOB, SO *I'M* GOING TO DO SOMETHING ABOUT IT.

YOUR FAILURE WAS COMPOUNDED BY THE FACT THAT YOUR LONELINESS WAS FORGED INTO AN ARMOR HARDER THAN THE ONE YOU CURRENTLY WEAR. MIDNIGHT COULD NOT STEAL YOUR HEART, BUT MISS CLARKSON DID. AND THEN, AS MIDNIGHT, SHE BROKE IT.

AND FIRST, IT WAS LOVE, AND THEN SADNESS, AND ULTIMATELY PRIDE THAT CLOUDED YOUR JUDGMENT, AND ALMOST COST YOU YOUR VERY LIFE.

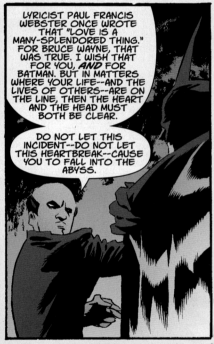

AND SO IT IS HERE, IN THE TROPHY ROOM, THAT THIS EPISODE WILL FOREVER BE REMEMBERED.

LYRICIST PAUL FRANCIS WEBSTER ONCE WROTE THAT "LOVE IS A MANY-SPLENDORED THING." FOR BRUCE WAYNE, THAT WAS TRUE. I WISH THAT FOR YOU, *AND* FOR BATMAN. BUT IN MATTERS WHERE YOUR LIFE--AND THE LIVES OF OTHERS--ARE ON THE LINE, THEN THE HEART AND THE HEAD MUST BOTH BE CLEAR.

DO NOT LET THIS INCIDENT--DO NOT LET THIS HEARTBREAK--CAUSE YOU TO FALL INTO THE ABYSS.

THE DEDICATION TO YOUR VOCATION IS UNPARALLELED; IT DOES YOU CREDIT. BUT IF IT BECOMES AN UNHOLY OBSESSION, AS IT DID WITH MISS CLARKSON, THEN IT WILL STRIKE YOU DOWN AND BRING YOU FAR LOWER THAN ANY PLOT THESE LUNATICS HAVE IN STORE FOR YOU.

LET THESE ITEMS SERVE AS A CONSTANT REMINDER OF THAT, *AND* A BEACON OF HOPE.

I'M AFRAID THAT SHE WAS ALREADY BEYOND SAVING, MASTER BRUCE. MISS CLARKSON HAD LOST HER WAY. SHE HAD LOST HER HOPE.

I HAVE READ YOUR FILES ON THE CASE, AND ON MISS CLARKSON. WERE I TO POSIT AN EXPLANATION, I THINK THAT APRIL'S DISCOVERY OF HER FATHER'S TRUE INTENTIONS WAS HER UNDOING. IT WOULD NOT SURPRISE ME IF IT WERE SHE WHO FIRED THAT BULLET INTO HER FATHER'S HEART. AFTER ALL, HER HEART WAS FILLED WITH HATE, NOT LOVE.

THEN... THEN LET ME ASK YOU THIS: I *LOVED* HER, SO WHY COULDN'T I SAVE HER?

TELL ME, ALFRED, WHY COULDN'T I *SAVE* APRIL?

THAT TERRIBLE DAY WHEN YOUR DEAR PARENTS BLED TO DEATH IN THAT FILTHY STREET, MY HEART WAS FILLED WITH HATE, AND I WANTED TO GIVE UP.

I FELT ALONE, AND YET MY DESPAIR WAS SHARED WITH THE ENTIRE CITY. *YOU* CHANGED THAT. FROM THE DETERMINATION YOU HAD WHEN YOU WERE A LITTLE BOY, TO YOUR UNWAVERING FIGHT FOR JUSTICE, YOU HAVE GIVEN THIS CITY *HOPE.* YOU HAVE GIVEN *ME* HOPE. AND THAT IS WHY I STAY.

BESIDES, WHO WOULD DUST ALL OF THESE COMPUTER SCREENS AND REMIND YOU TO EAT, WERE I NOT AROUND?

ALFRED... THANK YOU. THANK YOU, AND...

...I'M SORRY.

WE LIVE, AND WE LEARN, MASTER BRUCE. AS ALFRED LORD TENNYSON ONCE WROTE, "TIS BETTER TO HAVE LOVED AND LOST, THAN NEVER TO HAVE LOVED AT ALL." YOU MIGHT NOT AGREE WITH THAT SENTIMENT NOW, BUT I SINCERELY HOPE THAT, ONE DAY, YOU *WILL.*

NOW LET'S GET OUT OF THIS DRAFTY OLD CAVE. IT IS, AFTER ALL, A BRAND NEW DAY...

BONG!

It is midnight in Gotham City, and her citizens no longer live in fear that a monster will steal their hearts.

They are free to live their lives and enjoy the crisp night air.

But those who choose to terrorize the innocent and prowl the city streets without regard for the law--without humanity or compassion or hope--will have to answer to me.

I'm Batman.

THE END

AND SO THIS CASE IS CLOSED. THANKS TO STEVE, KELLEY, MICHELLE, PAT, HARVEY, AND JOE D. FOR ALL OF THEIR HARD WORK IN TELLING THIS TERRIFYING AND TRAGIC TALE OF WHAT HAPPENS TO THE DARK KNIGHT IN GOTHAM AFTER MIDNIGHT. THANKS FOR READING, GANG. UNTIL NEXT TIME, TRY TO ENJOY THE DAYLIGHT...
--MIKE

CHARACTER DESIGNS BY KELLEY JONES: **BATMAN**

MIDNIGHT

CLAYFACE

MAN-BAT

APRIL CLARKSON

JOKER AND SCARECROW

CLAYFACE

PROFILE

JOKERS EYES

CATWOMAN